Human Resources
as Business Partner

Human Resources as Business Partner

How to Maximize the Value and Financial Contribution of HR

Dr. Tony Miller

BEP BUSINESS EXPERT PRESS

Human Resources as Business Partner: How to Maximize the Value and Financial Contribution of HR
Copyright © Business Expert Press, LLC, 2017

First published in 2017 by
Business Expert Press, LLC
222 East 46th Street, New York, NY 10017
www.businessexpertpress.com

ISBN-13: 978-1-63157-905-9 (paperback)
ISBN-13: 978-1-63157-906-6 (e-book)

Business Expert Press Human Resource Management and Organizational Behavior Collection

Collection ISSN: 1946-5637 (print)
Collection ISSN: 1946-5645 (electronic)

Cover and interior design by S4Carlisle Publishing Services Private Ltd., Chennai, India

First edition: 2017

10 9 8 7 6 5 4 3 2 1

Printed in the United States of America.

I would like to thank
Cui Ling Lay and
Marcus Gee

From University College,
London & Chen Fuling
for providing the most up-to-date research information

Dedicated to all Human Resource professionals worldwide
who really want to make a difference

Abstract

This practical book sets out how HR can become a true business partner.

It will require a rethinking of HR's contribution to the organization in the future. All the key topics are covered in this work from a specific HR strategic model, reshaping of HR to align itself better with the business, and a number of new tools and techniques to aid in creating real financial value to the organization.

Many HR personnel have already jumped onto the title of calling themselves a business partner, but what this involves is a very different and complex skill set as well as a new process approach to creating added value.

Being a business partner is a very different and exciting approach to creating measurable value, specifically from HR activities and interventions.

Keywords

efficiency, forecasting, HR analytics, human resources, partnership, productivity, profitability, ROI, value, value added

Contents

Acknowledgments

HR has so much to offer any organization, yet it always seems to be the unsung hero, sometimes not recognized at all. New tools and techniques now enable HR to be a true driver of the three key elements that make up productivity; they are performance, competence, and reliability. These are all quantifiable and as such can be financially measured.

Being a business partner does require new skills and a very different approach. This is what's needed. But how to do it? Well, I hope this book will act as a catalyst in providing some useful help. I must thank the team of researchers and the many HR professionals from 35 different countries that have asked and aided me to put this book together and also the organizations that are putting all of this into practice.

Human Resources, The Business Partner— Introduction

There is a new feeling of optimism about the role and need for HR as a business partner. As a consultant I am fortunate to be able to speak with CEOs, CFOs, COOs on a regular basis; most are from well-known companies and are truly international. Their enthusiasm for HR is infectious—so why don't we see HR at main Board meetings, in critical planning meetings at strategy formation committees?

This is a question I have asked over and over again—the replies seem to be very consistent: HR is not seen as having

- Forward planning skills
- Knowledge about formulating business strategy
- The ability to produce financially measurable results

This book is focused on providing those interested with a how to do it approach to lift HR and to transform it into an effective unit with the capacity of becoming a true business partner and possibly a profit value center.

CHAPTER 1

The Challenge

1.1   Getting HR into Shape

The concept of redesigning the shape of New HR was an idea first expounded by Dave Ulrich. Before explaining this, it is necessary to cut through some of the myths in HR about who your customer is. Once that is understood a move to the new shape of HR becomes more comfortable and easier to explain.

I am fortunate in that I meet literally thousands of HR people every year. Ask them the question "who is your customer" and the reply is always the same (99 percent of the time)—the employees. But is this statement true?

It can't be—the HR function is a function that is funded at corporate level, the employees don't pay for the function, don't have any say about your salary, and they often use HR to undermine their managers. The employees have supervisors, team leaders, and managers to recruit, develop, and help them produce higher levels of competence and performance. It's also the line manager's responsibility to enforce discipline and deal with day-to-day grievance issues.

So what is HR's new role? It's a function to provide the tools, systems, and processes to enable managers to enhance and get the best from their staff. Using innovation and skill, HR can; if its focus is right, help an organization to significantly improve its performance. This is the essence of HR. The Business Partner.

To enable this to happen, HR will need to get into a streamlined shape so that it is in a position to take on more strategic and value-producing roles.

CUSTOMER and CLIENTS

HR Intranet

HR Call centre

HR Professional

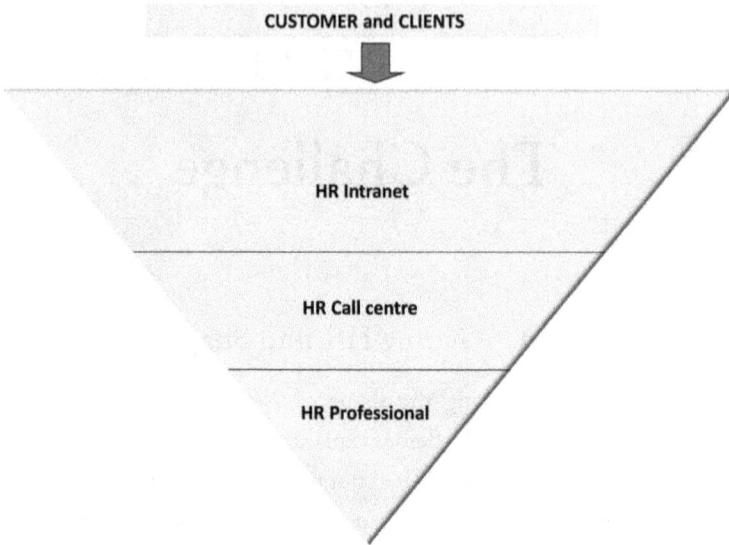

The concept is very uncluttered, put all of the terms and conditions, holidays, training requests on the intranet. Managers, staff, and employees' first point of information on any of these topics will be on your local intranet, cloud site, or system. The second line of contact will be by phone—these calls will be fielded by the HR call manager. This is not setting up a call center in the true sense but having a phone that is answered to deal with enquiries or for clarification about where to get information from. Invariably 90 percent of these calls will merely be directing people to the appropriate place on the intranet.

The third point or level of contact will be the HR professional—You.

This is where expert advice will be available and where you will be dealing with the senior personnel of the organization.

This design offers you many advantages. It will stop that endless stream of people wandering into the HR department and allow you the time to focus on what's important—creating value. It also sends a strong message to everyone—that you are a professional department and are running the function in a professional way.

I would also suggest, and this won't be popular, keeping the HR department door locked. This is necessary for a number of reasons. It's showing others that you deal with very confidential information and that you take personal security of employees' information very seriously. On this point alone you will get approval for doing this. Likewise as you will be working more on strategic plans you don't want anyone just walking in during a meeting or when you are producing organizational efficiency charts. It's a sobering thought that every one of your employees carries with them the perfect espionage tool—the mobile phone. A device that can record meetings, photograph sensitive employee pay details, and, with the right software, download corporate data in a trice.

So there it is; a performance-based layout for HR for starting to get into the right shape for the Business Partners' role. I'm not suggesting for one moment that HR specialists sit like gods in locked offices all day. They are best employed working more with the management team and senior managers on things like efficiency projects.

Work toward Being a Specialist

The second issue of what should HR be doing in the future is that of mastery. Although many of these areas of mastery will be discussed later in the book this will give you and the rest of the business a quick overview of the key areas of HR—the Business Partner.

1.2   The Strategic Focus and Process

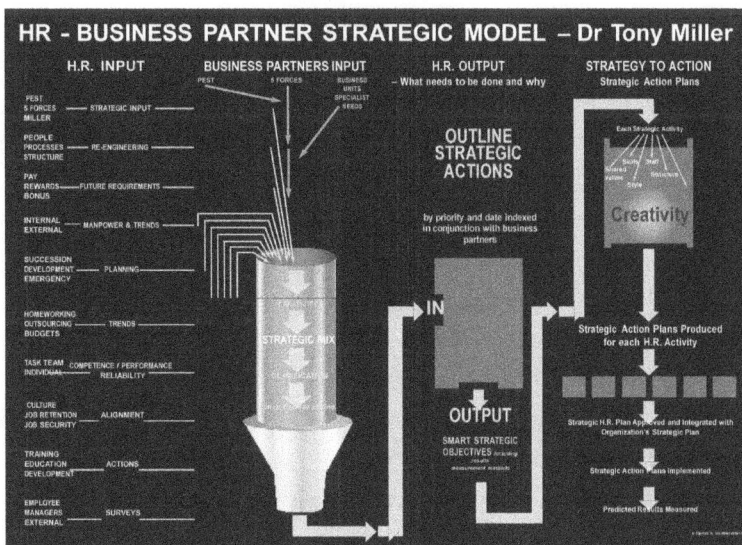

CROs and top management have repeatedly complained about the inability of HR to contribute to the formation of organizational strategy. This process map is an attempt to help HR to be more strategically focused using a proven template of what needs to be done. This process map also provides the vital link to lock strategic decisions into operation by using Strategic Actions Plans, also known as SAPs.

Strategic involvement for HR seems the inevitable development of this important function if it is to be a true business partner.

To date many HR professionals have found increased difficulty in trying to get to grips with current HR strategic models.

Most of their design, although well meaning, is oversimplistic and in the main does not provide the amount of critical information needed to collect and produce high-level strategic information.

This chapter is specifically focused on providing you with a complete map for not only putting together the HR strategy but also ensuring full integration with the business requirements.

Before getting to grips with the map, let's just spend a moment looking at timelines for the formulation of HR strategy.

There are three timelines we need to be aware of.

First, what we can learn from previous experience looking retrospectively at what we have done.

The second strategic timeline relates to current issues and information, which needs to be resolved in the future. The third and most important timeline is that of the future. It is only the future that we really have control of; from a strategic viewpoint it is the most important.

Often this timeline comprises both retrospective and current issues.

Most of the current strategic models that are being put forward for HR use are oversimplistic, particularly for those of us who are only involved in strategic planning occasionally.

Most businesses today use a model of some sort to ensure continuity and for putting strategic plans together.

The majority of these models consist of a combination of best practice in strategic planning and therefore use established strategic models such as PEST and FIVE FORCES.

In addition to those two models, there is the MILLER model, which looks specifically at productivity over time.

This model is essentially an HR model but tends to be reviewed by the majority of the other strategic partners.

The MILLER model, although being a strategic HR model, is specifically aimed at detecting when organizations need to change or reinvent themselves. Therefore, it has added importance for use in HR departments as it is HR's responsibility to point out strategically when change in the organization needs to be triggered.

The additional information not covered in the aforementioned three models is that of the strategic partners' specific area of expertise.

As well as using these strategic models, each partner will have a checklist of what to look at and report on for the future in their next strategic plan.

From what I've been told by hundreds of HR professionals internationally, this is the area that current HR professionals are having most difficulty with.

The map included here gives you a checklist of some of the most important HR areas to examine and use to see if there needs to be a specific inclusion in your strategic plan for those items. We tend to split our future focused plans into three timelines—each one has a very different type of approach.

Ferrari strategies: normally 1 to 2 years ahead, these are fun and most people can do them, often they are coupled to one specific financial year. This issue is with such strategies they do not have sufficient future focus; therefore, be cautious if all your strategies start to look like Ferrari strategies.

Oil tanker strategies: less exciting but when you start strategic planning for the first time—try to put forward more oil tanker strategies than Ferrari. The timeline for these is 2 to 5 years. You do need more effort and skill to use this.

Finally, Space Shuttle strategies 6 to 15 years. You really have to be a master of what's going on with the ability to grasp the big picture and to have the commitment to identify and see through such strategies. Longer-term strategies require a lot of very careful project management if they are to be delivered on time and within budget.

Having worked through the checklist and drawn up your strategic plan you can see from the map that there is then the strategic mix; HR strategy does not stand on its own.

It is part of a far more complicated strategy, as it has to integrate with the corporate strategy of all of the other business partners.

It is therefore extremely likely and from my experience inevitable that HR strategy will need to be reworked a number of times before it is ready for full integration into the overall business strategy.

Our HR strategic map may at first sight seem very complicated.

It is in three parts, Strategic Input, Strategic Output, and Business Plans for Action.

You will see that all of the business partners input their strategic requirements in the form of PEST, 5 FORCES, and their individual strategic requirements into the strategic mix. The latter are extremely specific to the strategic partners' own function.

On the map you will notice that we have highlighted the areas that are the specific function of the HR professional.

We hope that this will help you with the requirements needed to formulate your HR strategic plan.

The specific input for HR into the strategic plan takes the form of the 10 indicators.

HR input—10 steps: how many of these are specific to workforce management?

1. Strategic input—this consists of all three strategic models: PEST, 5 FORCES, and MILLER.

   The PEST analysis is a long-range tool. It is used to identify

   Political/legal issues

   Economic

   Social trends and changes

   Technology—innovations and change

   5 FORCES

   Competition among existing firms

   The threat of new entrants

   The threat of substitute products or services

   Bargaining power of customers

   Bargaining power of suppliers

   MILLER

   The MILLER model simply looks at organizational maturity over time.

Because organizations grow and productivity increases with time, this happens up to a point, after which the organization goes into decline. At that point the organization typically employs too many people, is too procedure bound, and does not produce enough output.

The position of the organization or department is found by using a questionnaire, which gives a plot on the MILLER curve. This model is the number one predictive tool for organization change prediction, and a copy of the questionnaire to be used by the managers is included for your use in the book.

2. Reengineering

What HR processes need to be changed—what will be necessary and what will the impact be? What HR actions in the strategic plan might require process change, what are they and, what is their impact?

Will the reengineering impact on any of the following?

People—will we need to change the number of people we employ in the organization to fit the new process? What is the value of the saving?

Process—the physical process. How will we implement the process change and how will it be carried out? What is its value?

Structure—organizational structure needed to support reengineering and people, process, or changes brought about by the indicators in the MILLER model.

3. Future Requirements

Pay—what pay levels are likely to be in the marketplace? What do we need to do? What are the financial projections?

Rewards—is the allowance and benefits scheme competitive, what actions are needed to change? What is the cost and the real value to the individual and organization? Would rewards be better consolidated into either higher pay or bigger bonus schemes?

Bonus—projected cost. Is the scheme right for our business—are we getting the productivity we need? If the bonus scheme is to be changed then what is the cost, projected productivity improvement, and an indication of our position against our direct competitors?

4. Workforce and Trends—These need to be predictive trends that will cover things such as sickness, inclusion, productivity, demographic, skills shortages, turnover, longevity in employment, speed to competency, organizational shape, etc.

5. Planning

   Succession—key personnel succession plans, desirable succession plans

   Development—trend/cost—speed competence, speed to performance, training needs

   Emergency—contingency plans for people in an organizational emergency, involvement of retired people, universities, other resources.

6. Trends

   Home working—what are the current trends and how will they impact on organizational structure, pay and conditions, and productivity?

   Outsourcing—identification of areas of the business, activities, and processes that could be outsourced. Return On Investment (ROI) and organizational implications

   Budgets—forecasting for HR budgetary requirements to meet strategic objectives for manpower. To include salary, training, allowances, and bonus payments

   Ageing workforce—what plans for the future—greater life expectancy and increasing retirement ages being imposed in Labor Law.

7. Performance/Competence

   Task—business performance trends via a Monte Carlo simulation, staff turnover, project approach impact on productivity, initiatives to improve productivity, competent trends projected, competency strengths and weaknesses by department

   Individual—competency/performance trends

   Team—introduction/expansion of teams/team types and productivity projected gains.

8. Alignment

   Culture—progress with the alignment of the corporate culture template will stop suggested actions/amendments needed depending on the suggested strategic objectives and the final strategic requirements

   Job retention—effects of job retention in the future, market trends, change in organizational shape, use of talented development techniques

Job security—techniques needed to give employees security and connectivity with the organization. May include share options, development programs, long-term contracts.

9. Actions

Training—training budget required for future, ROI on training, training efficiency relating to productivity. Training efficiency relating to competencies. External and internal trends on training

Education—educational standards required for the future, need to invest in education and second degrees. Link between educational standards and performance at work

Development—career development needed for the company. Internal and external trends in development. Development strategies for succession planning within the company

ROI figures for development effectiveness.

10. Surveys

Employee—satisfaction surveys relating to be linked between current state and future state of the corporate culture

Managers—surveys with the managers of the company to check cultural alignment and satisfaction with the working environment in the company

Any actions, which may be necessary to take for the future.

External—any evidence where external surveys have been conducted may show an impact on HR strategy, for example, type 2 diabetes, smoking, longevity of employment, etc. What actions are necessary for the future?

These 10 subject headings provide a sound basis for the organization input needed from HR. The 10 subject headings provide the initial HR input for the first part of the strategic input.

The Strategic Mix

The next stage is where the business provides its requirements (Business Partners Input) and during consultative meetings the HR strategic plan needs to be put into alignment with the overall business requirements and needs to reflect a total picture of what is required.

This approach avoids the embarrassment of HR going to the strategic table with no ideas and nothing to offer. It also clearly shows the business that HR is being a clear strategic thinker and able to devise and propose strategies that are truly strategic.

This map has only been in existence for a few years and already HR managers are reporting that other areas of the business are keen to draw up identical maps showing their specific strategic inputs.

Strategic Approval

Once the strategic blend has been completed final plans can be made and submitted for approval. Once approved the task of turning strategy into action commences.

Strategy into Action

There are a number of ways this can be done. Using the six S method seems to work best for HR strategic plans. This is shown on the strategic map.

Each HR strategic action (should be written as either a SMART objective or use the WWW model) will need to be translated into a strategic action plan with its resource and cost.

These plans can all be integrated into a comprehensive HR business plan for the short, medium, and long term.

Constructing HR strategic action plans gives you the perfect tool to upload all of the plans into one integrated process using something like Microsoft Project Manager.

The entire strategic plan of the business can then be run and operated as a major project with all the discipline of a major project.

The Role of Creativity

Specifically referred to twice on the strategic map, creativity needs to excel during strategic planning. This is a key skill for the HR Business Partner to master. The whole process of the strategy gives us a unique opportunity to be creative in the way that we would write and carry out our strategic plans. Creativity is an essential requirement of the HR Business partner.

Competitive advantage certainly will not be achieved by blandness or copying or following what we have done in the past.

In such a fast-changing world we should focus our attention very much on improvement or, what is more exciting, doing things completely differently.

A very simple idea to follow is the FACE approach not only to internal customers but also external customers.

The face principle requires us to deliver processes and concepts that meet its requirements. These are:

Fast
Accurate
Cheap
Easy

In addition, I am again reminded of Peter Drucker's advice to always ask the question "Would the roof cave in if we stopped doing this altogether?" The Virgin group completely scrapped their holiday process, deeming that employees could work this out for themselves.

We must make sure as a strategic partner that we do not create processes or activities, which significantly take energy away from the business.

That means radically reexamining lot of processes and trying to either abolish them or modify them so as not to take up valuable human capital time and effort. Our quest as HR professionals must be to energize and focus the Human Capital to maximize its potential and therefore achieve significant competitive advantage. Effective and creative strategic processes are a major step in the right direction.

Conclusion

This strategic map has been produced following many requests from HR professionals around the world.

It's not intended to be a map that you follow doggedly, but as guidance to you if you have difficulty in pulling all of the necessary strings together for strategic planning. It is unique as it provides a complete end-to-end process from strategy to action. In companies that have used this map (worldwide) the HR function has been seen to be a leader and other areas of the business have quickly adopted this process with great success and at the same time providing a companywide universal process.

1.3   The Roles within HR Have Formed into Three Areas

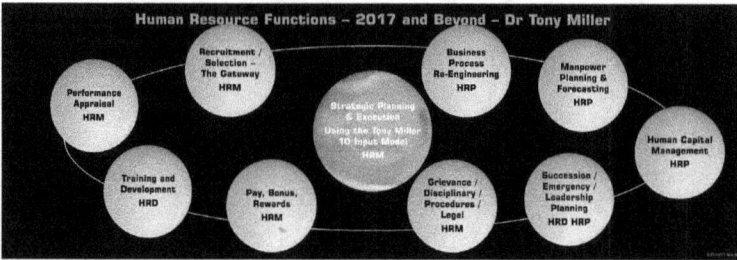

Human Resource Functions – 2017 and Beyond – Dr Tony Miller

HRM (human resource management) is the strategic arm of HR, which encompasses budgeting, strategy, legal, compliance, and HR policy. A recent add-on is human capital management, sometimes referred to as human asset management and of course pay and rewards. You will notice no mention is made of the legal part of the model. HR law is now so complex and specialist it should be completely handled by a qualified legal specialist—regardless of cost.

The second function of HR is HRD (human resource development). This covers training and education as well as the necessary actions for development and succession planning. In this function of HR all of the activities should be measurable and must provide measurable added value to the business. HRD is one of the easiest functions to turn into a profit center and has the potential for developing masses of added value. A simple challenging question to ask yourself about training is, "is this training added value to our business—if so can it be imperially measured?" If the answer is no, or if you are not sure—what's the business basis for doing the training?

The third and without doubt the fastest growing area of HR is HRP (human resource planning). No, this is not a new name for the old manpower planning. HRP encompasses:

- HR process reengineering
- Predictive planning and results prediction
- Succession planning

- Market employment analysis
- Organizational structure redesign
- Emergency planning for staff

This map of what the HR does looks spectacular when produced as PVC-covered large wall chart. It is a great aid in explaining to others just what HR does—believe me, many managers and an alarming number of CEOs seem to have very little idea.

1.4   New Skills Needed—HR as the Business Partner and Consultant

As a business partner, while you will apply your technical expertise, whether it be in HR, project management, systems design, training, or financial planning, be aware of the constant and potential dangers of assuming that as the expert you know all the answers, thus forcing your solution onto a client regardless of their own views. HR process consulting demands that you focus not only on the problem but also on your client, and you will need to be able to judge the right time to be at either end of this continuum. The reality of most organizational problems is that there is never one right answer to solve a problem. There are always several options that might be applied. Consequently success in the consulting process involves getting to one of those solutions. More importantly it involves getting your client to the solution that they feel most committed and comfortable with. Achieve this and you are likely to gain immense credibility with your client. Recognizing when you need to challenge your clients and when you need to step back are key skills that have to be developed. So learn to balance the expert and process role.

What Is the Difference between the Internal and External Consultant?

The classic story of the external consultant who borrows your watch to tell you the time, charges you for it, and then keeps the watch is perhaps a little exaggerated, but reality seems to suggest a lot of evidence for the caricature. We are all familiar with the problems associated with external consultants who enter organizations displaying huge amounts of arrogance, who all too frequently believe they know what the problem is before even asking any questions.

This form of behavior characterizes the worst form of consulting and frequently results in an enormous waste of time, effort, and resource. Of course, there will always be good and bad external consultants. It also seems likely that there will always be opportunities for good external consultants to thrive. But too often the solution to a problem already exists in an organization way before the arrival of any external consultant.

We have probably all had experience of organizations that are too dysfunctional in the way they are managed to listen to their own people when it comes to diagnosing problems and developing solutions. Despite the prevailing wisdom of some leaders, people who work in organizations do generally know what the problems are. They also understand the underlying issues and have the ideas to fix them. Regretfully, their views and ideas are all too often ignored or dismissed. One of the central themes of this book is to challenge this depressing convention. Indeed it might be argued that it is too often with the leadership of an organization where the problem really lies when it comes to encompassing new ideas and processes.

Internal consultancy provides an exciting and alternative option to these classic but highly frustrating situations. Consultancy is an operating style that aligns itself to the demands of flatter organizational structures and highly skilled knowledge workers.

But in exploring the nature of internal consultancy it is perhaps useful to begin with a comparison with external consultancy as this can help to highlight critical aspects of the role. In examining differences between the two it is not our intention to set one group against another but to simply recognize that there are key differences. As an internal consultant these differences should influence how you ultimately market your services. You will see from the list below that some of the differences can be used to aggressively promote a case for using internal consultancy as opposed to adopting the external route. At the same time there are some issues that will require you to examine and question your own skill set.

This question of objectivity is often a major reason why clients may seek external consultancy assistance. In some situations you may well find yourself competing with external consultants for a project. You, therefore, need to have a clear view of the relative advantages and disadvantages of either approach in order to shape your business case and proposals.

High-Performance Business Partner Skills—External Consultant:

- Able to learn from their clients and use this learning with other clients.
- Not emotionally involved in their clients' problems—they have no history of investment in the situation and can therefore be more objective and critical in reviewing situations.
- Independent—this is of course debatable—given that someone is going to be signing a bill.
- Often investing in new approaches and methodologies—they have to have something new to offer clients.
- Not always required to live with the consequences of their work.
- Not always being entirely honest when they say, "we've done this!" What they often mean is that "we haven't but we have really great people and expertise and we are really confident we will find a solution."
- Capable of developing a sense of dependency from their clients— "we cannot function without you now."
- In a business themselves—they are selling people and time and are interested in consultant utilization and profit maximization.

Internal HR consultants are:

- Employed full time by the organization.
- Likely to understand the overall business better than external consultants.
- Sometimes more knowledgeable than external consultants. You should know your business and industry extremely well. You may also have developed an approach or methodology that is ahead of any external consultancy group.
- Normally part of a specific function—Information Technology, Training and Development, Finance, Business Development, Internal Audit.
- Aware of the right language and culture of the organization. You know how things work and how to get things done.
- Able to identify with the organization and its ambitions—as employees you have a big emotional commitment.

- Liable to being taken for granted or lacking the credibility of some external consultants.
- Prone to being too emotionally involved in an organization—thus perhaps influencing your ability to be truly objective.
- Required to live with the consequences of their advice—you are still around long after the external consultants have left.
- Able to spread their knowledge and experience throughout the organization—you can enhance your organization's overall capability.
- Required to redefine past organizational relationships—the move from "colleague to client" requires a period of adjustment.

1.5   Your Audit of Your Consultant Skills

There are 11 key skills needed to be a good internal consultant. Rate yourself against these skills on the following pages and devise for each (if necessary) a plan to develop and improve yourself:

1. Personal image and interpersonal skills. How do you look, behave, and appear. How good are your listening skills, communication skills, and skills when running and chairing meetings?
2. Sales and marketing. Can you sell ideas—do you have good sales techniques (NLP)? Have you a plan to market your skills?
3. Business awareness. Do you know what the key performance indicators are in your organization? Can you calculate ROI; do you know your own costs?
4. Problem solving. Do you have a range of techniques that you can adopt to solve difficult issues?
5. Creativity. How do you rate your own creativity? Do you use established techniques to aid the creative process in others?
6. Financial understanding. Do you know your own unit cost, the cost of others? Can you compile and run budgets, forecast the cost of projects?
7. Credibility plan—built on successful actions not words.
8. HR-specific professional skills. Are you an expert in HR, in all the 10 key areas? If not what's your plan?

9. Forward planning. Have you got the necessary skills to do forecasting on trends, correlations, and to use predictive data?

10. Professionally qualified. Do you consider yourself to be professionally qualified in HR to be seen as an internal consultant?

11. Project manager. Do you have the necessary skills to set up, run, and deliver projects, on time and within budget?

1.6   Being in Touch with Your Organization—Critical for Success

The development of HR is interesting to chart.

In the beginning were Administration departments. The big change was the introduction of Personnel Departments, where functions primarily carried out were administrative activities, mainly payroll. Then as time moved on they got involved in other matters, mainly of an administrative nature. Despite what Personnel functions say they are mainly told what to do—told when and how many to recruit, told when and how much to pay people, so communications to this department tended to be very one way.

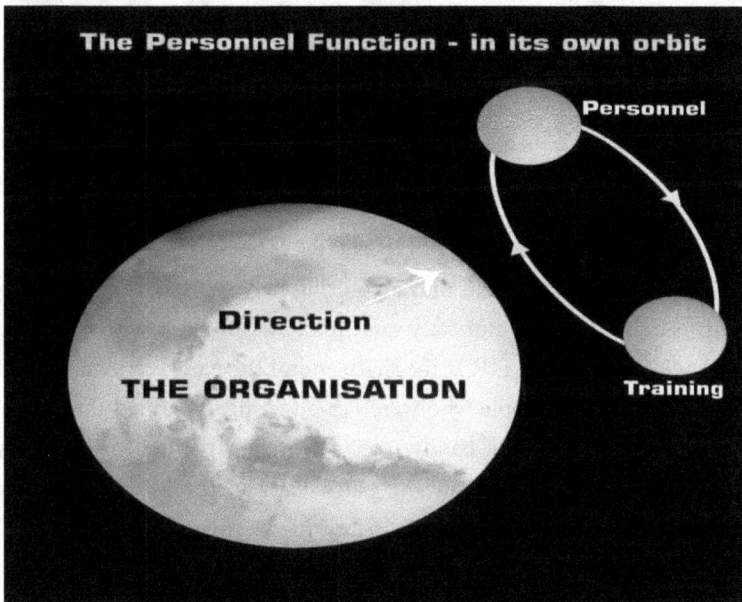

The Personnel Function - in its own orbit

Personnel

Direction

THE ORGANISATION

Training

The better qualified, capable, and more enlightened Personnel people decided that they should now be called Human Resources and this is the work that they should be doing. The problem was that at least 80 percent of the old Personnel function merely stuck a label on the door and declared they were now HR. Most of the real HR people did and have contributed to the business, but seemed unwilling or unable to produce strategic planes or to convert themselves into a value creation department. New skills, new software, and new attitudes were needed.

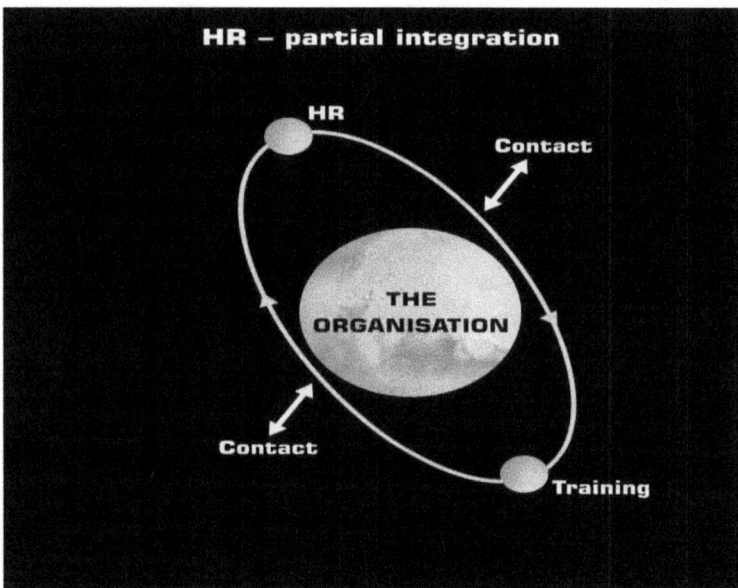

The current development of HR is HR—The Business Partner.

This is a brave and bold move requiring new skills and more importantly the ability to add monetary value to the organization by its activities and advice. This is real HR at the sharp end of the organizational arrow.

Regretfully the people who were Personnel people called themselves HR and jumped on the bandwagon convincing themselves that they are Business Partners. In addition, particularly in the Middle East, the awful title of expert has crept in: Recruitment expert, Training Expert, and Business Partner Expert. Most of the "Experts" I have met in the last year are seemingly average, which of course gets the real HR professional a bad name.

Chapter 7 gives a more detailed view of the work and skill set needed.

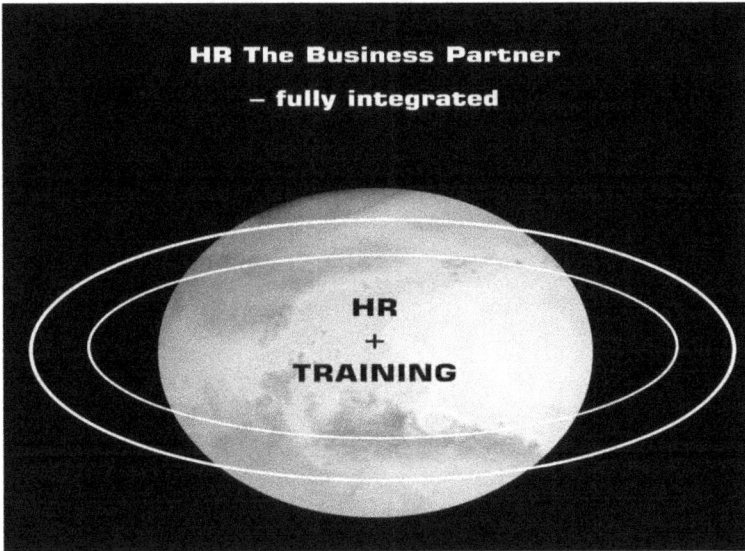

CHAPTER 2

Mastering Productivity

2.1 Productivity

Sustainable productivity comprises three key components. In HR we must fully understand the component of productivity and have clear strategies to improve in every area. This is one part of the business that if you make any improvement it will be truly welcomed and you will massively increase your credibility as a Business Partner.

It is all about collecting the right data and planning strategically how each of these areas can be improved. It is crucial that we get this critical data at least annually. The collection of the information is normally linked to the performance appraisal cycle.

The first and perhaps the most obvious of these components is competency. The second area is that of performance and the final, and probably the most neglected, is the area of reliability.

A word of caution about the collection of the data:

$$\text{Competence} + \text{Performance} + \text{reliability} = \text{Productivity}$$

Both competence and performance figures normally come from the performance appraisal process. It is very important that you are aware of the statistical significance of collecting this data so that it can be of use to the organization and for your own processing needs. You need to collect all the data so that it's shown on a 1 to 100 scale. In other words, you need exact numbers.

Many organizations use simple tick box systems, which are a poor design—easy for the managers to use but useless for statistical analysis and forecasting:

Unsatisfactory   Below average   Average   Outstanding

In this commonly used method the manager simply ticks the box where appropriate, either for competence levels or for performance.

The problem then is the range—unsatisfactory covers a numeric range of 0–25, below average 26–50, average 51–75, and outstanding 76–100. For accurate modeling and forecasting this is just not accurate enough. So for all your data collection design systems and processes, give exact numbers, preferably on a 0–100 linear scale.

This is necessary for new workforce planning in all its areas of data collection so that future data manipulation and comparisons can be made.

2.2   Competence

The topic of accurately measuring and valuing competencies has eluded both line managers and HR personnel for years. The numerous books to explain competency frameworks have done nothing but to add complexity and confusion to what is a very simple concept.

What Are Competencies and How Are They Structured?

The concept of having a competency framework was to enable organizations to benefit from a uniform approach. Competencies are a key observable behavior. There are very important words in that short statement—the first is key. When allocating competencies to a job the focus needs to be on the key competencies; the first and most dramatic mistake organizations make is to allocate as many competencies as possible to cover every single item of work. By so doing, it makes the task of measurement unattainable. Be practical, just focus on what competencies are critical or key to the job, then the task of measurement and doing training needs analysis becomes attainable and realistic.

The second important word in the definition of competencies is behavior. We can see, measure, and improve behaviors as they consist of skills, knowledge, and experience.

Having a proper competency framework provides organizations with three important outcomes. Competencies provide us with:

- Quality assurance
- Conformance to standards
- Doing things in a safe and legal way

Without such standards, it is easy to see how mismanagement seeds economic downturns. The current economic downturn is a classic example.

The abuse and misunderstanding of how competencies work has meant that in many organizations their overcomplicated approach has significantly reduced productivity. In an attempt to rectify this we have set out from scratch how competency frameworks should work as they can be a positive contributor to productivity and more importantly have credibility with the business users. Regardless of what approach you take or which model you use, simplicity and clarity of approach are essential if you are to maximize your investment in your employees.

To get the most from a competency approach, managers need to fully understand how competencies work and why they are important. From practical experience, it comes down to each employee having no more than eight competencies, with six being the average. Key competencies are the ones that really make the difference.

In order to make this clear there is a complete worked example.

The illustration shows how a Team Leader competency is constructed. The smallest elements are seldom individually rated and training for these parts typically occurs on the job. In the illustration, the competency unit is of key interest as this is what we measure and provide training for as need arises.

The organizational requirement of competence is important from a training needs analysis viewpoint. Although competence affects every individual, the requirement for competence has already been scoped, approved, and funded at the corporate level. Therefore, although competencies appear to be an individual training need, they are really part of the organizational requirement that guarantees and gives conformance to organizational standards.

From a training needs analysis point of view, competencies are challenging, especially when the competency does not quite match a training course or packaged solution. Identifying the appropriate

Elements	Unit

Delivering results and Quality

Monitors progress of individuals

Avoids bottlenecks in work

Refers issues upwards quickly

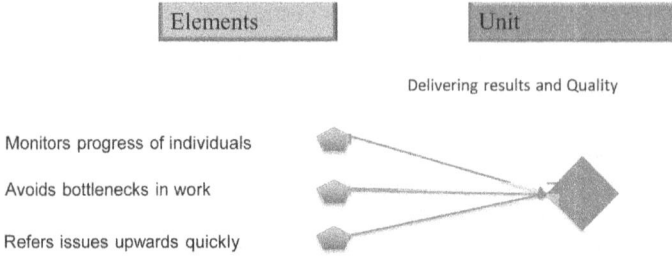

The all important units and their relationship to the competence.

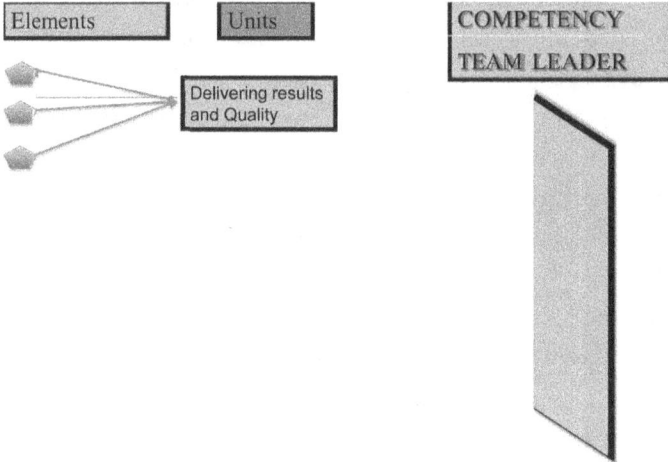

Elements	Units	COMPETENCY
	Delivering results and Quality	TEAM LEADER

The competency framework

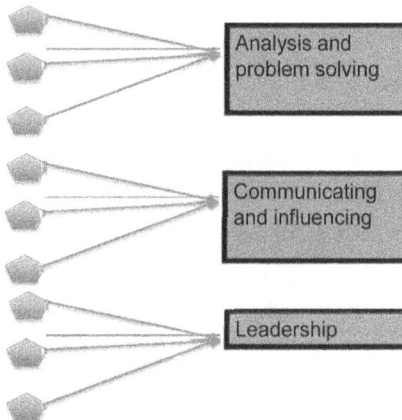

Analysis and problem solving

Communicating and influencing

Leadership

The all-important units and their
relationship to the competence

training to achieve a higher level of competency is subject to broad interpretation.

Before embarking on an exploration of training needs, minimum and maximum standards need to be set for the competency framework within your organization. Although it is unlikely that you know, right off, the minimum, average, and maximum competency levels required in your organization, these data are essential when you conduct your training needs analysis. For example, if the minimum competency level is 50 percent, the average competency is 70 percent, and the maximum competency is 85 percent, then you can clearly identify the priority for the training needs analysis resulting from the competency level of the individual. This is normally recorded at performance appraisal.

Competencies comprise three parts: the competency itself, the units that feed into the main competency, and smaller elements that lead to the units (see illustrations). This might sound complicated, but in practice the concept is incredibly simple and works well. In performing training needs analysis, or establishing the competence of a person, the most important and efficient part to consider is training at the unit level because that's where training and development has maximum impact. In the example below, you can see what the units are for the Team leader—just four.

Team Leader Competencies

Competency Unit	Definition	Anchor
Delivering Results and Quality	Directing effort to the achievement of objectives	Ensures satisfactory team delivery of defined goals, overcoming most problems within own area of specialization
Analysis and Problem Solving	Analyzing information effectively and drawing sound conclusions	Evaluates available information, reaching decisions based on key facts and practicality of solutions
Communicating and Influencing	Achieving understanding or gaining acceptance of ideas and proposed action	Prepares case fully, stressing the benefits to be gained and inspiring confidence in own views
Leadership	Getting the best from others	Monitors progress toward achieving clearly defined shared objectives; provides feedback, support, and encouragement to individuals on specific tasks

2.3   Setting and Measuring Competency Results

Measuring competency levels and getting the best from training.

What's the competitive advantage of this approach, e.g., focusing on measuring only units? First we need to be realistic about setting organizational competency standards in line with the KEY competencies. In the illustration, the minimum competency standard is set at 50 percent.

This sets the bar for future recruitment—it ensures that all recruitment is competency based and that training is only given to employees who score below 70 percent at annual appraisal. This will also feed into minimum scores for any bonus scheme. The information is used on the HR productivity dashboard and can be projected using a Monte Carlo simulator to predict trends.

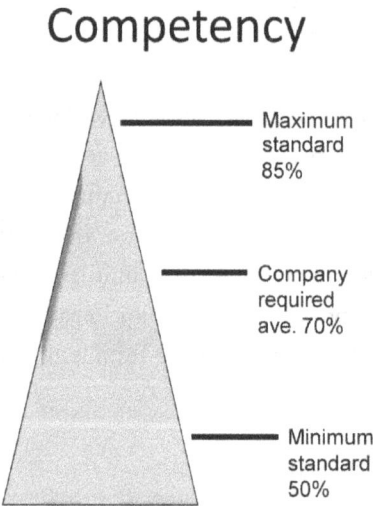

Competency

Maximum standard 85%

Company required ave. 70%

Minimum standard 50%

It will also show the organization its strengths and highlight any areas for remedial activity. As competency-based training accounts for 98 percent of the training budget, using this technique will help to produce accurate training budgets.

2.4   Performance

Introduction to Performance

Performance is raw output, essentially how much we do. Performance is measured in a number of ways including:

- Speed
- Time
- Efficiency
- Unit cost
- Volume

What performance is expected should be very clear in the contract of employment, although companies should seek legal counsel in this regard as employment law statutes vary geographically on this issue.

On the other hand, performance levels above those required should be locked into a bonus or reward system. If the original criteria are correctly set it should be difficult for employees to do more in the same time, since in theory they are working at their optimal level. So you will need to make the decision—bonus or overtime—but not both.

Performance expectations (above required performance) should be established during the performance appraisal and updated throughout the year.

Measuring performance can be done in three different ways. These are approached depending on the type of business you work in, the country you are employed in, and finally the culture of the company or organization that you are a part of.

1. Performance measure by time worked. This works well if you have managers who really do manage. Also certain cultures are very work focused and when they are at work—they work really hard. This particularly applies to China where hard work by the hour is part of the culture.
2. Performance through individual target setting. This is a real winner but it carries with it a big warning. Properly set and monitored targets with big bonuses produce massive results, provided:
   a. The end of the year the bonus is not subjected to forced ranking
   b. That the bonus must be subjected to the average competence and reliability scores being achieved
   c. That the bonus is directly aligned with organizational achievement.
3. Performance through team target setting. Very much the same criteria as the above but using a Hopper Bonus scheme where all participants (The Team) need to meet the score requirement for competence and reliability before any bonus can be earned.

Companies that take their eyes off of this soon find themselves in real financial difficulty. There are three approaches to get performance; each has its own advantages and disadvantages. Self-motivated staff—these employees are painstakingly recruited and just know what needs to be done. They require little motivation or supervision and work whatever hours are needed. They are normally bounced via some form of share/stock option scheme. The second is the managed workforce—employed but not trusted. Management runs a strict and inflexible routine. In this instance, performance is achieved by hours worked, the manager taking responsibility for prescribing work and making sure it's done in the time allocated.

The third and most abused is the setting of objectives and stretch targets. The old style managers are just not good at doing this and are constantly undermined by having forced ranked bonus schemes determining who gets what bonus at the end of the year.

2.5   Measuring Performance

Consistent theme in performance—it must be measured.

Regardless of which of the three schemes you use, the approach for measurement is the same as for competency. Management needs to set minimum company standards, and top-end figures for performance.

Performance – preset standards

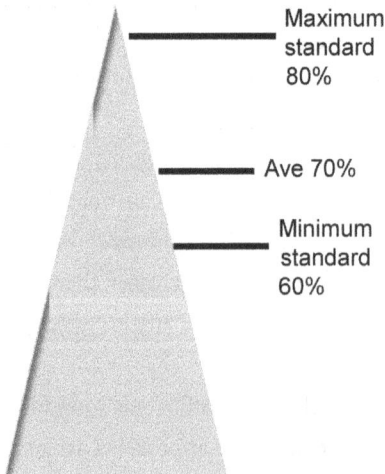

Maximum
standard
80%

Ave 70%

Minimum
standard
60%

As with competency (quality), no bonus or additional payments should be made for anything below required average standard. In fact, if required performance is not achieved, then employees' basic salaries ought to be reduced. Check this out carefully as it may not be legally possible although I think it's morally right. All of this highlights the need for thorough recruitment practices, just look at how good Google is at this—and look at their bottom line performance figures.

You may be wondering why productivity is not at 100 percent in our chart. Well there are two very separate components that affect this. The first is TIME. In a 38-hour week—no one can work 38 hours; we have PT&C time plus a lunch break. So at best the working week will only be 30 hours of available time.

Poor overall performance is then compensated for (by the Managers) who demand more staff—resulting in overstaffed organizations.

2.6   Reliability

Reliability is a dimension of value that is very rarely measured by workforce management. So what is reliability and why should we take it seriously? We already know the costs of an employee and what that cost is per day. We also know the cost of an employee per hour. Reliability is a measurement of whether or not that person works for the hours that they are paid.

Unreliable people tend to commence work late, often leave early, and have a remarkably high level of unsubstantiated sick leave.

The two key areas for us to focus on are sickness and unsubstantiated days off (either from uncertified sickness or from other reasons). Although this sounds more like absenteeism, for our purpose—we call it reliability.

Other areas of unreliability are also important but the main ones are those highlighted.

Why we need to get on top of this is because it costs lots of money directly and has a negative effect on employee morale indirectly. That is why measuring reliability is increasingly an important factor in workforce management and reporting the cost of unreliable people is a major business cost factor.

Fortunately, mathematically, it is now possible to calculate by individual, section, or department the direct cost of reliability. We have developed a formula for this; this can also be projected using our predictive workforce management tools showing the cost over 5, 10, and 15 years. For all organizations, this figure is so significant it cannot be ignored.

2.7   Measuring Reliability

If we look at an example of one person coming to work late every day (just 30 minutes) they have 14 uncertified sick days in the year, then what is the cost in reliability for that employee for one year?

$$£46 \times 0.5 \times 226 = £5,198$$

$$£46 \times 8 \times 14 = £5,152$$

$$\text{Total cost} = £10,350$$

If 20 percent of our 3,000 strong workforce falls into this category then the real cost per year is $600 \times £10,350 = £6,210,000$ DO I HAVE YOUR ATTENTION NOW?

So for our three time scales of 5, 10, and 15 years that's:

$$5 \times £6,210,000 = £31,050,000$$

$$10 \times £6,210,000 = £62,100,000$$

$$15 \times £6,210,000 = £93,150,000$$

From work on reliability carried out over a number of years these are very conservative figures. If this does not grab your attention—then do the calculation based on Birmingham City Council's figures:

$$100 = 0$$

$$75 = 96.5$$

$$50 = 193$$

$$25 = 289.5$$

$$0 = 386$$

17.9 days off each year for each of the 50,000 people.

When gathering data we use formula 2 and then the figures are converted into a linear scale so that we can correlate them for other comparative work if needed.

Using your facts you can now do a benchmark to find out how reliable your employees are and what's the cost to the organization. It's management's job to rectify the fault if you have a big issue here—not yours. You have identified the problem—costed it and provided the management information on the cost to the organization. Ongoing monitoring will make this a key Human Capital measurement factor.

It would be prudent to come up with a figure of where you expect the organization to be on the chart—100 percent is not realistic.

Thus in 2012 using an existing formula (the Bradford formula) we have mathematically adjusted the output so that the output scale runs on a 0 to 100 scale with the indicators showing when counseling is needed, when a first verbal warning is given, when the first written warning is given, when a written warning is given, and when a final written warning and dismissal are given.

Using a new piece of software it's now an integrated package, which can be used, with competence measurement and productivity measurement.

The data are fed into this program and the appropriate actions to be taken are displayed to the manager so that there can be no oversight, slippage, or ability to "forget" to take action.

As I mentioned earlier, reliability is one of three key indicators, which together equal productivity. It is important that any decisions on increments, bonus, allowances, or promotion are only taken viewing the total picture. Very often reliability is not taken into account during interviews or for selection and promotion. Poor reliability has a marked effect on other employees' motivation. To such an extent this is a serious impact on organizational efficiency if it is left unchecked.

Financially the cost of poor reliability is enormous. Not only in straight financial terms, e.g., the person's salary but also in terms of missed deadlines, slippages, and lower quality standards. Therefore, I'm sure you can see that reliability is a key indicator and essential for our dashboard.

Can poor reliability be identified?

Significant evidence exists that likely poor reliability can be shown using personality profilers.

Other research has been carried out looking at the impact of job satisfaction and absenteeism and this seems to be clear evidence of positive correlations between high-frequency absenteeism (many short absences from work) and dissatisfaction in the job.

This further shows the importance of doing regular staff satisfaction surveys to insure and measure the relationship between absenteeism and the staff satisfaction scale. This is so important that it features on our dashboard productivity indicator scale.

Projections of Lost Time through Poor Reliability

Using formula 2 and the appropriate software is possible to get a linear numeric score (0–100) that shows reliability. By then modeling the data using a Monte Carlo-type simulator you can project the reliability factor for 5 to 10 years in the future and then establish what the financial costs will be to the organization. Then you can strategically develop a plan for improvement, which can be financially measured.

2.8   Reliability and Recruitment

Reliability is very important when recruiting. Reliability—if an important part of the job should be identified on a Personality Profiler. High Conscientiousness scores are good predictors of reliability. Failure to find this out on recruitment can have serious consequences for the very best of workforce plans. This was revealed in 2012 when G4S, a security company, had been awarded the security contract for the Olympic Games—hosted in the UK. The recruitment process was flawed and the complete lack of testing for reliability produced headline news in most of the UK papers as staff failed to turn up for work.

The following information was printed by the Daily Mail Newspaper on July 15, 2012.

Just four of the 58 staff expected to report for duty at the Hilton Hotel in Gateshead, Tyne and Wear, showed up, one of whom later disappeared.

Use of the Three Pieces of Data

Using the software the three data streams from competence, performance, and reliability are modeled to show if the person has achieved the minimum requirement—if so then is the appropriate trigger for entering a bonus scheme, being eligible for an increment, or being considered for development.

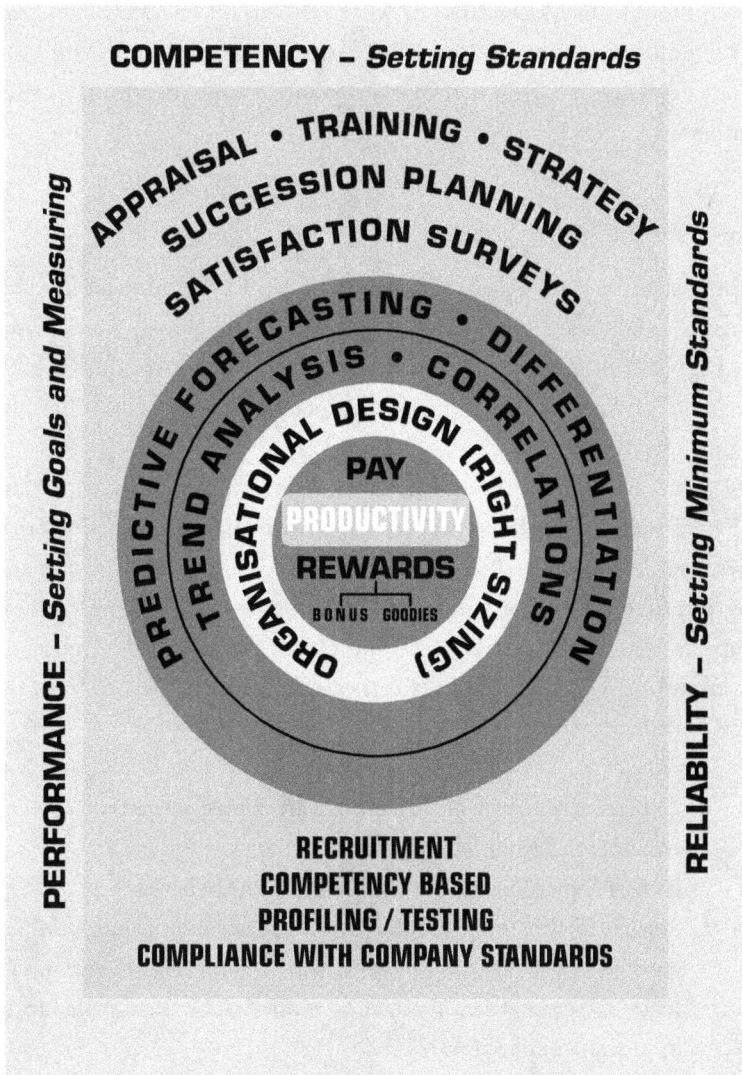

Key Business Partners' Activities

Historic Development

The concept of HR having key performance indicators has been around for a long time. It was started in an attempt to bring Human Resource Departments in line with other business areas and to try to get the old style personnel departments more focused and accountable for results. Many of the consulting companies were quick to jump on the bandwagon offering their own "products" and trying to define— even though they knew little of what HR should be accountable for. The result was never completely successful as it failed to provide concrete evidence to CEOs that HR really added value in a fiscal quantitative way.

Case Study Example

The best current example of HR evolving from Key performance indicators to a dashboard system is that of Sysco in the United States. Sysco is a supplier of food for the catering industry in America and is a great example of where HR is in good alignment with the business through being a real strategic partner.

Sysco has a number of Dashboard indicators—all of which are aligned with the business strategy. One of the dashboard actions that Sysco looked at was staff turnover. Improving the staff satisfaction and by improving compensation to align it better with the individual's expectations, turnover reduced. Specifically what did this mean on bottom line results? Specifically this was the financial benefit from the HR action.

- 75 percent of Sysco's operating costs are people-related costs, which amounts to $3 billion each year.
- It costs approximately $50,000 per associate who leaves.
- Sysco's HR function was able to make a massive contribution which resulted in the company moving from a 65 percent retention rate to an 85 percent retention rate. In money terms this equated to an improvement of $50 million.

2.9   What Does the Dashboard Do?

The dashboard provides a highly visible indicator of how HR (and key business indicators) is performing against their yearly targets. To do this it has, just like a car, critical indicators specific to HR but critical to overall business success. This has an equal application to the Public sector.

The dashboard used here focuses on five key areas, the two most critical being the first two, comparable to the car speedometer and rev. counter.

The productivity dashboard is a significant leap ahead for HR and is far more in tune with what is done to produce real organizational results. The first move in this measurement many years ago was the Key performance indicators. They were a good start—bit just like competencies the process rapidly got overcomplicated as various consultancy companies sought to "Sell" the system—warts and all. Working with key performance indicators can, if one is not careful, work against the total benefit to the organization.

Two examples where KPIs failed the organization:

Financial Services Company
The Sales Director of this company that sold insurance had a KPI to increase sales by 6 percent in one calendar year.

The target was achieved—the Director got a substantial bonus. In the next year the renewals fell by 10 percent —the people did not like the pressure selling that was taking place. There was a lack of joined up thinking linking sales to retention although it was 2 years before this was picked up.

Large Manufacturing Company
Another example of where disconnected KPIs have an adverse effect on business performance. One of the KPIs, of the training function, was to complete 9 days of training on average for each employee and to spend the agreed budget. In the same year the operations function were targeted with improving output and reducing head count.

In this company operations did not release anyone for training to do their very demanding KPI—and also fell short of their target,

Meanwhile in the support functions of the business many employees were forced into having 25 days training—the training function met their KPI!

If KPIs are used their approach must be well orchestrated and a clear view of what the organization requires need to be clear to everyone to avoid mismatches in effort.

Progressing forward, the best example of using this dashboard approach is Sysco. The value they are able to demonstrate on a year-by-year basis using this system is amazing.

The process has been refined and at the same time retained its simplicity allowing organizations to take a Do-it-yourself approach, setting their own target levels depending on the industry, country, and economic climate.

Dashboard—The Three Productivity Indicators

We have previously discussed Competency, Performance, and Reliability and know that we can measure all three. One of the great strengths of the performance dashboard is that it's put on display in each department, so you can see at a glance how you are doing throughout the year against the target scores or presets.

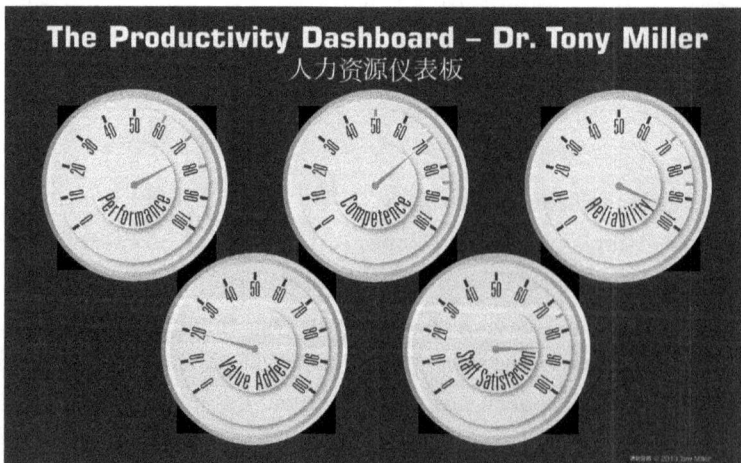

The Productivity Dashboard – Dr. Tony Miller
人力资源仪表板

Just to recap:

Competency gives the organization quality, safety, and conformance to standards

Performance gives volume, speed, output, low processing cost, and agility

Reliability gives attendance, value, minimum head count, and dependability through stability

These three measures give us that all-important productivity.

Other Indicators—Staff Satisfaction

There is a lot of evidence to show that high levels of staff satisfaction reflect in low turnover, and often but not always, higher productivity.

Measuring staff satisfaction is therefore a critical factor in our dashboard.

A word of caution here—be careful not to be overzealous and overdo it, once a year should be ample, less if you are in a period of rapid change.

Most organizations prefer to design their own surveys, make sure you are satisfied; it will give you the evidence that you need and that the results are available on a 1–100 score as previously discussed. If you want to buy in a ready-made solution you could use one of the more generic products such as the SHL corporate culture lite.

Once the survey has been completed over a number of years you could start doing correlations with the survey results and see how they relate to the three productivity drivers: Competency, Performance, and Reliability.

It is unlikely that Workforce planning will be involved actually doing the surveys, but the scored results are a critical part of our data collection needed for various correlation exercises.

Added Value

What is added value? It's the value you can demonstrate above total cost. We use Formula 9 HR and training ROI.

AV (actual business value created in one year) – total cost of activity = added value (or loss)

Workforce planning is the perfect department for becoming an added value function, therefore a profit center; closely followed we hope by the other parts of HR—including those in HR who are the business partners.

The value is measured in one year so that it is directly linked to most organizations' budgetary cycle. HR has to change due to two major influences, the changing quality of people and a growing need to measure human capital and to develop that capital into a measurable strategic business advantage. People are constantly improving; we have higher education standards, and greater literacy and a high level of competence with work-related IT. This makes today's employee vastly superior than at any other time in history. Today's employee therefore needs less management control and less process control to work effectively. Given that backdrop it's essential that HR in all its facets alter to reflect these changes.

Businesses now want a human resource department that can add value. A profit center rather than a burdensome cost. Logically, if HR is a major player in all things related to our greatest cost and asset—people, how could it possibly be a cost center?

The chart sets out to set the standard for the current financial year. In the example on the chart we have the added value target preset at 20 percent.

If that preset was for the entire HR function then the added value it would need to show would be a contribution in one financial that was 20 percent over total cost. It's up to you to decide at what level you set the bar, start off at a manageable figure—say 5 percent and move upward as you gain confidence and succeed.

CHAPTER 3

Our Employees Are Our Greatest Asset?

Who does HR work for? The straightforward answer is The Directors or senior management team. It is this group that provides the budget for HR to function and it is this group that pays HR salaries; they are the prime customer and should see the financial ROI on all HR activities.

It's a key function of HR to improve the Managers and supervisors by providing techniques and processes to assist them to improve productivity and efficiency of their departments/teams. In doing so successfully, HR becomes the business partner.

3.1   Understanding Differentiation

It was Jim Collins, the author of Good to Great, who came up with the very profound statement:

"Our employees are not our greatest asset—the right ones are." After you have read this section you will see why he is so correct.

The concept of differentiation was first used by Jack Welch and is mentioned in his books specifically:

"Winning." Different groups of people are paid in categories according to their productivity output. In a survey carried out in 2013/2014 of large organizations—Department/Divisional managers were asked to reply to two questions:

1. What is the percentage of Talented, Average, and Poor performers in your department?

The second question

2. Based on a 40-hour contracted week how many hours of real work do each group do in the week?

The answer to question one

Talented people—Estimated number in the organization 17 percent
Average people—Estimated number in the organization 61 percent
Poor performers—Estimated number in the organization 22 percent

The answer to question two

Talented people hours worked 32 hours
Average performers hours worked 22 hours
Poor performers hours worked 5 hours

If we look at poor performers first, there are some interesting observations:

- First, who recruited them?
- Why are they still employed?
- How much money have we squandered on them?
- Have they had any pay increases at all? If so why?
- What is the cost of unauthorized absence and sickness for this group (it's always the highest)?

When addressing these issues it's so clear that once it's written down and costed that the three groups should be paid completely differently (differentiation).

Poor performers need to be paid as little as is legally possible—with absolutely no other benefits. Average performers no more that the basic salary plus training.

Talented people—pay a lot with massive bonus schemes.

Now old style HR people feel very uncomfortable with this so we need to explore a few of the basic issues with poor performers.

3.2   The Basic Cost of Poor Performers

All the calculations that follow are based on a real company, which employs 3,000 people. In nearly all workforce planning work sooner or later you will need this calculation.

Part One: How many days do people actually work in your organization, normal reply 365, but it's not true, so how many days do your human resource work. The calculation will vary from company to company, an acknowledged average is 226 days a year. When you use the formula you will need to adjust the figures for an exact fit for your company.
Formula 12

$$\text{Days in the year } 365 - (\text{Holidays } 25 + \text{Public Holidays } 10 + \text{Weekends } 104) = 226 \text{ PWD}$$

The figure of 226 becomes the amount of days for productivity calculations, business expansion, or contraction calculations and the basis of calculating the employee standard unit cost (ESUC).

What Is the ESUC for Days Actually Worked?

The ESUC is the basis of all calculations for efficiency, production costs, and efficiency savings. This is one very emotive figure, once you understand how it's calculated then run it past the finance Director to get the figure approved—remember this is a rough unit cost, it's an average—not an exact figure. It's good enough for us to do a range of calculations and predictions.

A Worked Example of Formula 5

This company employs 3,000 people with a total salary bill that includes salaries, overtime, car allowance, housing allowance, and ALL allowances including medical and any tax contributions. In this example it amounts to £125,280,000.00.

You will see on the calculation that the total salary costs are multiplied by 2. Two is our real expenses we can attribute to every employee training, electricity, facilities, IT, floor space, company vehicles, etc.

If you have lots of spare time, you can work this out by looking at the annual accounts (private sector only) but for simplicity we use 2 as the factor. There are a few companies where the factor would be higher such a Google, Apple, Facebook, etc.

Remember you are not the company mathematics department—you just need working standard figures.

We then divide the top line total by the number of employees, which gives us X.

Understanding these two formulas 5 and 12 enables you to take a hard look at what people do in the time they are actually available for work.

ESUC. To find the Unit cost for any employee per day
Part 1

$$\frac{\text{Total salary + associated costs}}{\text{No. of employees 3,000}} \frac{£125,280,000.00 \times 2}{} = £83,520 \text{ X}$$

X is then divided by 226 (PWD) to give you the ESUC per day, which is the true cost of each employee in the organization.

$$\frac{(\text{X } £83,520)}{226} = \text{ESUC } £369 \text{ divide by 8 (depending on Country) to get hour rate } £46$$

I have experienced little comment on calculating the PWD, but the ESUC always seems very controversial, often the comment from CFOs is that it is not the way we do it—my reply is always the same to this statement—"well please show me the formula you use" —of course there is not one.

Part three
Calculations for the poor performers lost cost
22 percent are poor performers so out of 3,000 employees that's 660 employees
660 poor performers × hourly rate ESUC £46.0 0 × lost hours per day 7× work days in the year

$$(\text{PWD}) 226 = £ 16,446,472.00$$

Addressing poor performance is now a key priority and it financial impact on the company can be clearly seen. If you want to look at the total cost, add in some of the other factors mentioned in 3.1

Who will support you in your strategic actions; the CFO will be a very active business partner and your major ally.

3.3   Linking Differentiation to a Bonus Scheme

It's one thing having a differentiation idea—putting into practice is another matter with such major differences in International labor law. The trick, if there is one, is to design a process that is transparent and one that will be automatic. The process that fits differentiation well is our hopper bonus scheme—this locks into the HR dashboard as previously discussed.

The Productivity indicators provide an input for your bonus scheme. Using the three presets: Competency:

70 percent

Performance: 75 percent

Reliability: 95 percent

With this input data you can use a hopper-type system to feed a bonus scheme either team based or individual based.

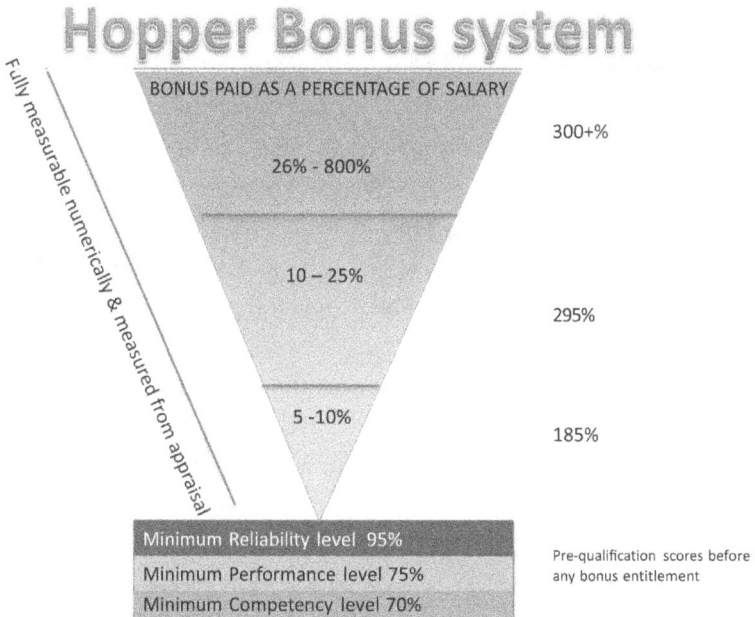

Hopper Bonus system

Fully measurable numerically & measured from appraisal

BONUS PAID AS A PERCENTAGE OF SALARY

26% - 800%

10 – 25%

5 -10%

300+%

295%

185%

Minimum Reliability level 95%

Minimum Performance level 75%

Minimum Competency level 70%

Pre-qualification scores before any bonus entitlement

If you fail to meet any of the minimum scores they are excluded from the scheme and any other enhancement to the basic salary/wage. This is a very fair and equitable way of putting a scheme together as the rules for entry are very clear. Earning bonus is then decided only on the performance scores, as both competency and reliability are the minimum quality assurance figure.

This used in conjunction with the performance dashboard provides management and employees with the "rules" needed to participate in the bonus scheme—if you want more all you have to do is to increase your Performance score once to have achieved the minimum qualifying score.

3.4   Managers Need Help

Performance and dealing with poor performance is an area we could put in more effort and the value added created would be amazing. This would primarily be a job for training provided they could provide the quality necessary to produce real results in the workplace.

As with competency (quality), no bonus or additional payments should be made for anything below required standards. In fact, if required performance is not achieved then employees' basic salaries ought to be reduced. Check this out carefully as it may not be legally possible although I think it's morally right. All of this highlights the need for thorough recruitment practices, just look at how good Google is at this—and look at its bottom line performance figures.

You may be wondering why productivity is not at 100 percent in our chart. Well there are two very separate components that affect this. The first is TIME. In a 38-hour week—no one can work 38 hours, we have PT&C time plus a lunch break. This situation is worse if you look at the three categories of employees:

- High performers will work productively for 32 hours each week.
- Average performers work for about 20 hours each week.
- Poor performers work for only 5 hours each week.

The data for hours worked were obtained from a large survey carried out in 2014/2015 of over a 100 large companies mainly in the Middle

East. Managers seem completely unaware of the difference between being at work and actually doing work.

This is one of the biggest reasons why most companies are overstaffed by 15 to 20percent and of course much higher in the Public Sector. Published figures in late 2009 by the government in the UK showed that there were 50 percent too many people in the Public Sector, and specifically in the public health service it was reported by McKenzie Consulting in September 2009 that 1 in 10 employees in the Health Service could be dispensed with. In a survey of Public Sector Employees in September 2009, 89 percent felt that budgets and Public Spending were managed inefficiently.

What performance is expected should be very clear in the contract of employment, although companies should seek legal counsel in this regard as employment law statutes vary geographically on this issue. On the other hand, performance levels above those required should be locked into a bonus or reward system. If the original criteria are correctly set it should be difficult for employees to do more in the same time, since in theory they are working at their optimal level. So you will need to make the decision—bonus or overtime—but not both.

Performance expectations (above required performance) should be established during the performance appraisal and updated throughout the year.

Beyond SMART Objectives

Triple W objective setting © This system was designed by Dr. Tony Miller in 2011. Recognizing that managers and supervisors just did not apply SMART objectives he used knowledge from his strategic mapping process to come up with triple W objective setting.

The Basic Concept

Most objectives are a result of strategic requirements and strategy focuses on three main areas, what needs to be done, why it needs to be done, and finally when it needs to be done. That applied, and you get all you need to set very clear and easy to understand objectives.

The Process

The first W is the what, what is it that needs to be done, or what is it that needs doing. This needs to be spelt out so that its clear to understand. Example:

To improve productivity in the back office by 20 percent this year (that's before the triple W process).

What is required?

- To increase the number of case files dealt with by 20 percent a month, that's 50 extra, 600 extra in a year.
- The work is to be locked into a project program on our Microsoft office management system showing all the deliverable, dates, and number of extra files processed—the exact numbers to be shown for each month.

  Why? Without the why the person doing the objective will never fully understand the context of their objective and why, if they have this information they may be able to produce a better way of doing it.

- In order for our company to be competitive we must increase our volume but without incurring any extra costs, such as more manpower.
- The timing will be crucial as the sales force have very specific targets to achieve and this will directly affect our workload commencing on the 1st October this year. Everyone should be aware this is a priority as it is a key element of our strategy.

  Finally the When: It is critical here to be specific. Don't just give an end date. Anyone who has managed projects will tell you that that's asking for slippage. So take time to break the objective into manageable chunks. Dates given should be by day, month, and year. Where figures are involved, try not to use percentages but exact numbers—this will avoid confusion or any misunderstanding.

- This objective fits in with the department strategy for continuous improvement and innovation by demonstrating its efficiency improvements over the next 5 years.
- The plan for achieving this is required for outline approval by April 2, 2011 and must be agreed and approved by May 1, 2016.

- The first batch increase is needed by October 1, 2017 (50 files) and the total objective is to be completed showing the 600 extra files by October 1, 2018.

One of the greatest assists to performance improvement is any business using this system to ensure things get done on time and within budget.

Managers and supervisors only require a short but focused piece of training to be able to do this—remember there is a vast difference between the managers saying they can do it and the reality of well-written Objectives.

You may be wondering in the Triple W objective method why there is no explanation of how to do it. With today's workforce people are bright enough to work this out themselves or to find out. If they take the objective on board and work out how to do it then they will be more committed and accountable for the outcome as it's their idea. This simple but effective approach really does produce results and more importantly gets a lot more commitment to action.

It's important to give up the notion that people will automatically improve or that performance/competency problems will sort themselves out. This just does not happen in today's business world; therefore, quick action that is helpful, effective, and decisive is required.

Get into a productivity-focused mode as a state of mind, a way of thinking things through. Always surround yourself with good people and carry this process through in all your recruitment efforts. Harv Eker, author of Secrets of a Millionaire Mind, reminds us, quite appropriately that, "If you swim with the ducks, you can't expect to fly with the eagles." Should you need further convincing, we highly recommend Bob Pritchett's book, "Fire Someone Today" in which he shares several illuminating examples.

Performance is our key tool in turning HR into a profit center—it's not just getting people to work harder or smarter—we have a very real job to do in making sure managers have the right tools and process to make this happen. We also should seek out and destroy any processes or practices that take energy away from people. The late Peter Drucker summed up this approach very nicely when he said, "Would the roof cave in if we completely stopped doing this?" Many times we seem to have processes that don't add value but do absorb a lot of time.

CHAPTER 4

Organizational Design, DownSizing, and Right Sizing

4.1 Organizational Design Historical Development

It was in 1760 that Adam Smith set out the ideas that would shape businesses. He made the first symmetrical designs for how an organization should look and designed the first modern organizational structure; a company called Arkright in Cromford in the UK first used it in 1771. Then it was adopted by a factory called Smedley in 1784 which is still going—officially known as the world's oldest factory.

Then it was adopted as the model for success by other companies worldwide and surprisingly this structure for organizations is still very much in evidence today.

Smith was also responsible for the new business titles of Supervisor and Manager and for the recommendation that the ideal span of management would be 1:7. This was appropriate in 1760—despite the technological and education revolution there is still a belief that people require close supervision and must be managed.

These two factors, old organizational design and 1760 supervision, have condemned us to the productivity and efficiency problems we have today. So why do so many managers and supervisors still want small ratios of control? The reason is that it's less work for them and requires less skill; but it then begs the business question—what do we pay managers for? It is estimated that 95% of existing businesses are still structured on the design principles of 1760 and the pioneering work of Adam Smith, capability and type of work undertaken. This is still the predominate design in the world today as it's easy to do.

4.2   The Three Current Types of Organizational Design

Symmetrical Organizations

The 1760 Adam Smith design, used by most average companies in the world, is simple, traditional, and easy to work out layers of pay, gradings, and promotion ladders. Layers in the organization can sometimes be 14 deep and in today's fast-moving and fast-changing world this design is really out of date. Symmetrical organizations are however the best organizations to downsize.

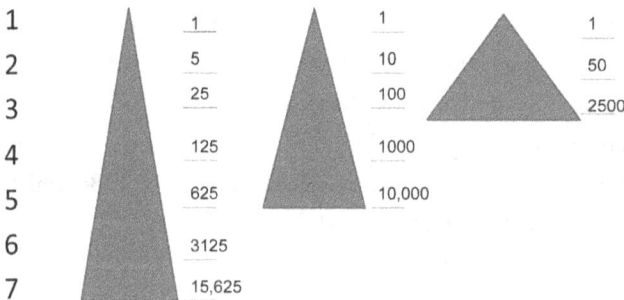

1	1	1	1
2	5	10	50
3	25	100	2500
4	125	1000	
5	625	10,000	
6	3125		
7	15,625		

Spans of control and organizational shape

Asymmetrical Organizations

The Asymmetrical principle does not stick to the same ratios of supervision to employee, but has different ratios for different levels and parts of the business, depending on the role, capability, and type of work undertaken. It's a much better and commonsense approach to organizational design and will always work where the organization employs a mixture of average and smart people. It is difficult to pinpoint when this design first became used, but I guess it was in the late 1960s. The design has many advantages as it allows parts of the organization to have a very flat structure, while other parts are more in line with a Smith type setup. For the HR business partner this type of structure has so many advantages in cost and efficiency its certainly worth exploring as the main rival to the symmetrical design. Many Financial services that have call centers use this design with great financial benefit.

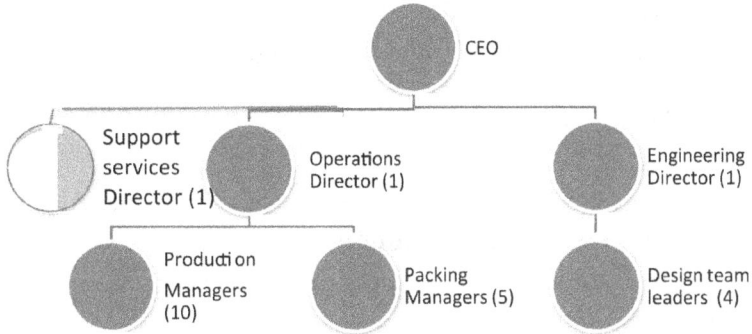

Asymmetrical

People Centric

It's hard to believe that the founders of a people-centric organization were all connected with the IT business and were nearly all scientists or IT engineers. Although the design is not new, Dr Miller first coined the term people-centric organization at the Balkans HR summit in 2012.

The start of the People-centric organization happened perhaps by chance and was a spin-off of the way William Skockley worked. Shockley was simply a brilliant man. He has been credited with the revolutionary work on the transistor and later advancing semiconductors. Shockley coinvented the transistor, for which he was awarded the 1956 Nobel Prize in Physics.

Shockley's attempts to commercialize a new transistor design in the 1950s and 1960s led to California's "Silicon Valley" becoming a hotbed of electronics innovation. In his later life, Shockley was a professor at Stanford. Thus, over the course of just 20 years, a mere eight of Shockley's former employees who formed Fairchild Semiconductors (named after its financier Sherman Fairchild) in Silicon Valley California later gave forth 65 new enterprises, which then went on to do the same. Shockley Semiconductor and these companies formed the nucleus of what became Silicon Valley, which revolutionized the world of electronics and, indeed, the world itself.

What Shockley had started was a new way of doing things and a new way of running efficient organizations based on a people-centric design; whether this was a design formed by analysis or by need we will never know—but the success of Silicon Valley speaks for itself.

The founding companies using this form of organizational design:

- Shockley Transistors 1950s
- Fairchild Semiconductors 1957
- Intel 1968—founded by Robert Noyce and Gordon Moore, perhaps the first company to offer stock options to all its employees and have the flat organization as we know it today
- Microsoft 1981
- Apple 1997
- Google 1998
- Facebook 2004

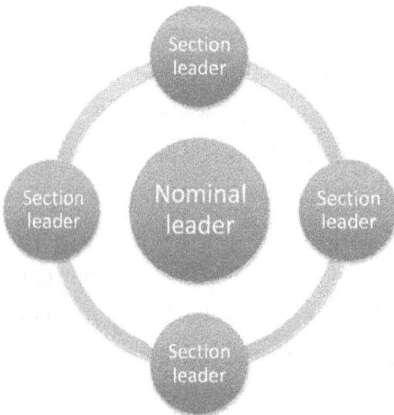

People centric

The people-centric organization is so different and is based on the concept that the organization should be designed and structured to get the best from the type of people it employs instead of designing a typical organization either symmetrical or asymmetrical and making the people fit the organization. If you are wondering if this works—take a look at the stock value of the companies mentioned.

The epitome of this design is Google. The organization was created to support those that would work in it—right from the start. The design was specific to meet the personality profile of Technological Engineers. What a change, instead of getting people to fit an organizational design, first deciding what people you needed (by profile) and then creating an entire organization to support that ethos. The design first became apparent in 2001 with the appointment of Eric Smitt as the new CEO. Google has always been good at recruitment (a lesson we should learn from); they had always valued people with high SAT scores and high grades from the best colleges and universities. You can't graft on mental horsepower so it's best to make sure you get it when you recruit.

The new Google organization had been created new, different, very functional, and almost free of bureaucratic rules which are endemic in symmetrical organizations—the skeptics of course said it would never work—just look at the track record of Google. This design innovation was quick to be copied by Apple, although the world at large has failed to capitalize on this type of organizational innovation.

The Future of Organizational Design

The future of organizational design will become a combination of asymmetric and people-centric designers, when re-engineering existing organizations will be subjected to a hard time, as all the existing managers will fight the change as the day of the conventional manager being essential has now reached a plateau. Many managers realize that their days are numbered and soon their numbers will inevitably decline.

When designing the organization or redesigning an existing organization remember that today people are educated to a very high standard, overmanage them and you will never see them reach their potential. Overmanaged people often find work boring and this creates a disconnect between the management and the workforce. This will become very apparent and will work against the organization if for any reason the organization has to change quickly.

To conclude—be bold with the organizational design, try not to use the past as a benchmark, the greatest strengths organizations have is the untapped potential of the employees—use the organizational design to capitalize on this.

4.3   Downsizing

Downsizing is a term used in workforce planning for altering significantly the structure of the organization. Normally it is done to both symmetrical and asymmetrical organizations at a period (midstage two) of the MILLER organizational maturity chart. Downsizing is a risky business as it involved taking out complete layers of management. Doing business process re-engineering normally but not always precedes downsizing.

The key to successful downsizing is to remove layers of management in the organization by finding out the answer to one simple question: Where in the organization is the work actually done?

Although the question sounds simple—it's often not that easy to find the organization. Every layer claims, "this is where the work is done."

Organization before delayering (operations functions only).

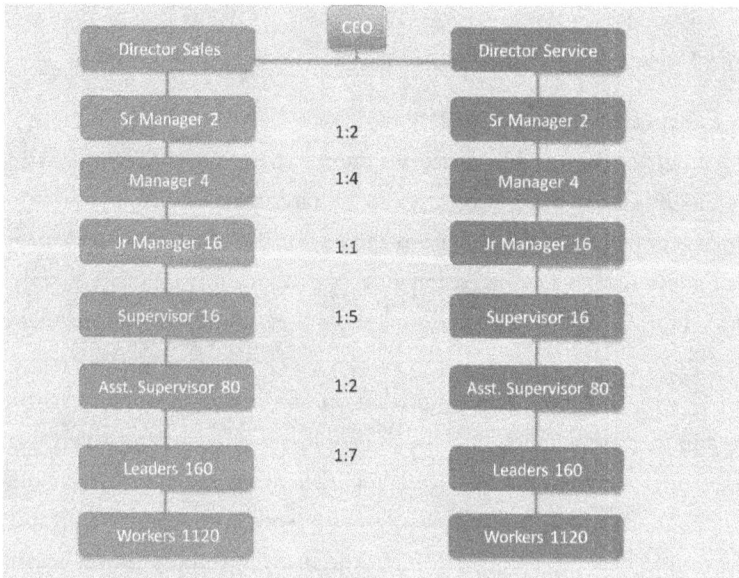

Once you have established the truth then you can go about removing layers and completely restructuring the organization by delayering.

Organization after downsizing

Benefits

- 28% improvement in productivity
- Less management
- Improved worker satisfaction scores

Although there are so many examples of this, recently British Airways delivered and took out of the structure 450 managers—it was reported "it had no operational impact on operational effectiveness." So the question is—what exactly were they all doing—a very expensive and unneeded overhead.

In the Public sector, Essex County Council removed layers of management, by twenty percent. Reported on BBC and available on You Tube, in an interview Essex County Council said "the reduction of management will have no impact on ECC front line services."

Downsizing is not without risk; my advice—employ a consultant who has done downsizing before and can provide evidence of its success.

4.4   Rightsizing

Rightsizing is a technique that is quick to do and involves using one of our mathematical formulas. Unlike downsizing it is almost risk free and gives very quick returns on investment. The methodology to do rightsizing is by using formula 10. How to do this is covered in Chapter 7.

The rightsizing exercise is always interesting to do as it give you a reality check on the size of the organization. Public sector organizations would be advised to do this on a yearly basis and measure the "rightsize" against the preset budget.

Rightsizing is quick, often from design to implementation it can be done in 4 months. Compare this to downsizing 1–2 years ago.

The main cause of organizations getting out of shape and oversize has been caused by two separate forces, Poor recruitment and lax Management. This combination has been shown to expand organizations and produce up to 50% more employees than is necessary. Getting the numbers right is a massive contribution the HR Business Partner can make.

The Traditional Method

When most organizations attempt rightsizing they tend to use the "Nibble" technique. Someone in the organization wants a more efficient organization so the game of playing with the structure begins. This is done in several ways but the most widely used is to nibble at the organization to reduce head count. This can be done by freezing recruitment, early retirement, or getting volunteers to leave with a golden handshake. Although this has been done for years, there is very little structure and science to this approach.

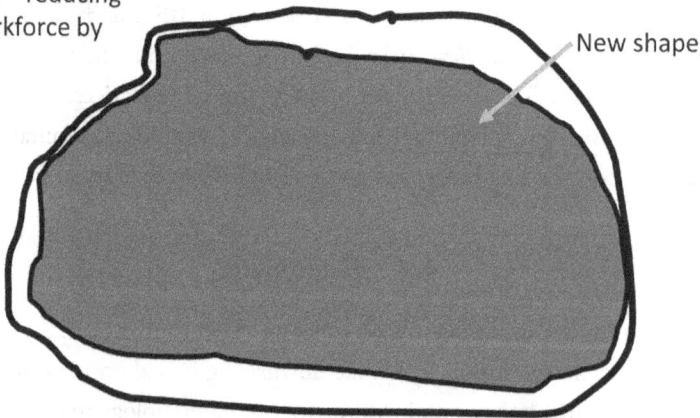

Deciding if this is the right size – reducing workforce by 5%

New shape

Has productivity risen or stayed the same?

Rightsizing

New Shape

New Approach—New Results

In 2015 the mathematics, process, and software were in place to rightsize and to do it as a tabletop simulation before committing to putting the plan into action. This has made the entire process very safe and predictable.

In this chapter, we will now explain the entire process end to end with all the data based on a European Company employing 3,000 employees.

Step One

The process must start with two questions for the CEO:

Q1 Are you reasonably satisfied last financial year most of the work in the organization was carried out?

The reply is normally a guarded "yes, I suppose so."

Q2 This is a quick question and you really want a fast response.

How many hours a year do our 3,000 employees work? They are contracted to work 40 hours a week.

The reply is normally given based on this assumption:

40 hours a week $\times$ 52 weeks a year $\times$ 3,000 employees = 6,240,000 hours a year

So we have it from the CEO that all the work is being done by 3,000 people working (and being paid for) in 6,240,000 hours.

This is the basis for starting our mathematical modeling for right sizing.

Step Two

We know a few facts already:

- The ESUC for this company is £46.00 per person per hour (formula 5); you will need your own data from your organization to get this figure.
- Employees in the company work 226 days in the year prime working days (PWD; formula 12); for this formula you must use the figures from your own company to arrive at the exact PWD.

So all the work is done using our HR formula as follows:

8 hours a day $\times$ 226 (PWD) $\times$ 3,000 employees = 5,424,000 hours

So we have immediately lost (what the CEO thought people worked and what we pay for)—our figures based on PWD

6,240,000 − 5,424,000 = 816,000 (difference between theory and reality)

Step Three

As in all organizations there are other lost time variables. In our test example company, we find for each employee:

Average time lost through reported sickness	10 days per year
Average unauthorized absence*	5 days per year
Average for Training/ conferences	12 days per year
TOTAL extra time lost	27 days per year per person

* This figure is normally on the low side as Managers often turn a blind eye to recording all unauthorized absence.

To rebalance our standard PWD figure we will need to make an adjustment.

Revised PWD 226 – 27 days = 199 days

We now have to do a recalculation based on the actual days worked rather than on the forecast.
Actual hours worked in our company:

Days 199 × Hours per day 8 × employees 3,000 = 4,776,000 hours

Now we have a really accurate picture which shows us what is actually happening; all of the work is being completed in 4,776,000 people hours—what a difference from our CEO guess at the beginning.

Step Four

As we know employees are in three categories—poor performers, average performers, and talented. We also know from a large survey done in 2015 how much work they do.

> It is critical for all workforce planning predictive calculations that you know in your organization the percentages of work in the three categories and how many hours they actually work in a day.

In our organization

17% are talented, total 510—they work 6.4 hours a day
61% are average performers, total 1,830—they work 4 hours a day
22% are poor performers, total 660—they work 1 hour a day

Talented PWD 199 × hours worked per day 6.4 × number of employees 510 = total hours worked 649,536

Average PWD 199 × hours worked per day 4 × number of employees 1,830 = total hours worked 1,456,680

Poor performers PWD 199 × hours worked per day 1 × number of employees 660 = total hours worked 131,340

Total hours worked per year 649,536 + 1,456,680 + 131,340 = 2,237,556 hours

Step Five

We now know all the work done in our organization was done by 3,000 employees actually working 2,237,556 hours although we are paying them for 6,240,000 hours.

The question the management team must address is exactly how many hours a day do you expect your employees to work. This may be decided by the CEO or it might end up being a Management team decision. Remember this is NOT the end of the rightsizing exercise yet.

In our example company it was decided that all employees should work 7 hours a day. Therefore going back to our original PWD is 226, the final calculation would be:

A) 226 PWD × 7 hours a day = Hours each employee is expected to work each year 1,582.

B) Now we are going to divide our hours per year for each employee into our actual total hours worked to give the number of employees needed to run our company.

$$\frac{2,237,556}{1,582} = 1,414 \text{ rightsized figure. Actual number}$$
$$\text{currently employed 3,000}$$

This figure is referred to as our rightsized base line figure. It is our base line for you to decide what numbers you would need to run this organization with a small safety margin.

What we have gained so far while doing this simulation is valuable management information that we will use to make our strategic decision on what to do next.

Information we now know:

- Numbers of Talented, Average, and Poor performers.
- We are in a position to show a financial case of the cost of poor performers.
- We can make a financial case for rightsizing.
- We have identified poor performers and know where they are clustered in the organization and who their managers are.
- We have a benchmark figure for new hours to be worked daily (7).
- We can decide at this stage if now is the time to move to a different organizational design.
- We have information on who we need to release and can draw up a proposal.

Step Six

Deciding on how many people you need—this is a Management decision—in the example we have been following, the organization had decided to go with an establishment of 2,000, as this was seen as only a medium risk strategy.

Removing people from the organization is in most countries very difficult. The groups who will never meet the new standards are the poor performers—they are your number one targets.

Other methodologies you may use could include:

- Early retirement
- A limited incentive to leave scheme but only for a short time

- Not filling any posts occupied by current poor performers.
- When your new organization chart is finalized the last push would be compulsory redundancy.

Financially the organization will be in much better shape and will certainly be much more effective. On the overall saving, there are sufficient funds to introduce a sparkling bonus scheme, by now you will have reenergized the organization and become THE business partner.

Step Seven—Producing the financial case

Showing the financial case is the most important factor in getting management approval. So let's look at the figures in our example that we would present to the CEO.

From step six we have decided to run the organization with 2,000 employees—releasing 1,000 people from the organization.

The group we would target is the poor performers and the bottom performing from the average group.

So let's look at the costs

ESUC £46 × 8 hours a day × 226 working
days a year × 1,000 employees   = £83,168,000

Training costs £125.00 cost per day × 10 days
a year × 1,000 employees   = £1,250,000

Cost saved in 1 year   £84,418,000

In this case study we have established that our company can be run using a total of 1,414 employees—this is an absolute minimum. In reality just over 2,000 people rather than the 3,000 that ran the company with the old establishment.

CHAPTER 5

Four Key HR Processes and How to Improve Them

5.1 Business Process Re-engineering

The need for HR process re-engineering—a critical skill if you're going to work with the business as a partner and focus on improvements.

The best educated workforce ever, dynamic Information Technology and systems, more employment law than ever before, the highest levels of training—yet why are we failing to get the performance increases we hoped for? Rather than chasing the latest fad or fashion we might to better to be a bit circumvented and look at what acutely takes performance from people. Most of our current performance problems are traceable back to the time of Adam Smith (1776) and his thoughts on how work was structured and managed. There are three major restrictors of performance in most of today's businesses; the Public sector is certainly included here.

1. The organization of work and the thoughts about the structure of labor created a management structure that can't possibly work in today's business environment. With today's highly educated workforce it is absurd to believe that management structure originally devised in 1776 could still be appropriate today. Yet many organizations still believe they need an army of supervisors to watch the workforce. Every supervisor is blessed with a manager and it's hard to understand what exactly managers do in today's business—one thing for sure they don't do added value work. So in the organization we have two positions, which are largely surplus to requirements if real performance is sought.

2. The second restrictor of performance is specialization of labor. Taking a job and breaking it up into many small tasks—and then further complicating things by having strict splits between departments.

3. The third restrictor, and at the same time the solution holder, is the process we devised to fit the circumstances surrounding items 1 and 2 above. Processes, however, unlike fine claret, do not improve with age. Aged process becomes a massive restrictor of performance, reduces training efficiency, and is a demotivator.

Processes are really organization orphans, everyone feels they ought to do something, but in reality very little is done to improve even key processes. The organization problem this causes is now easy to see. Human Resources are charged with getting the very best from employees—our most valuable resource, yet we have processes, which make the attainment of that goal impossible.

It's not difficult to see that the management of processes should be included in the HR remit.

Process management and improvement offer the organization the possibility for greater efficiency and to gain quantum increases in productivity. It fits well in New HR, as the process is directly related to improved performance and efficiency of people. New businesses often capitalize on this factor when they start, being faster and more efficient than their competitors. A good example is that of Direct Line, the insurers. This UK Company who were unknown when they started became the industry leader in under a decade.

Process management improvement sits well in the workforce planning function of a business-focused HR. Why, as it is mainly statistically and process based? Let's examine how this can be achieved and attempt to give you sufficient information for you to be able to practice on one of your own processes.

Getting started. The first objective is to pick a process that is 100 percent in your control. This will enable you to practice until you become sufficiently confident to move onto more complex processes.

Our process consists of five stages.

Stage 1. Identify the process to be examined—make sure you and whoever knows the process well knows exactly where it starts and where the process ends.

Stage 2. Measure and map the process—walk through the process at least twice, time and record exactly what happens: how many people involved at each stage, how long it takes, transmission time, delay time. The picture you are building is of elapsed time—this must be real and accurately measured. Elapsed time is exactly what it says. If I put something in my out-tray for you at 5 pm in the afternoon and you look at it at 10 am the next day the elapsed time is 17 hours. When measuring what happens—remember that employees have breaks, lunch, and have a start and finish time.

You are not attempting to find best performance in the process, merely record what happens on a day-to-day basis.

Mapping the process. In order that others and we fully understand the process we need to map out exactly what we have recorded. The maps we use are call swim lane maps.

These have the departments involved on the left with horizontal lines across the page segmenting the different departments. As you draw the map, each step moves to the right, so that you can see the time line involved. Under no circumstances move to the left to conserve paper (you can't go back in time). These need to be drawn up on large sheets of paper, as you will want to review and amend the map until you are sure it represents what typically happens.

Unsophisticated as it sounds—this is best done on the floor. We use symbols to make the mapping easier, once finished it looks rather like a wiring diagram, but is very easy to follow and see the total steps in the process, together with delays, hand-offs, and excessive checking.

Adding up all the time then gives us the Elapsed Time (ET) for the process. At this stage, there is little point in getting people to comment on the map, as it's just a representation of what exists now. If you are not familiar with the process you could get a signature on the map to confirm that's what the current position is. At this stage be careful you don't get given lots of ideas on how to make the process a bit better—that comes later.

There is an example for you to try—a simple example using the post-delivery for a small company—just to let you have the opportunity to practice.

Stage 3. Creativity and Innovation—Now we have our process map we need to look at what we are going to do to improve the process. This is the first trap we come to—doing this exercise is not about making an incremental improvement—it's about a complete redesign, starting from scratch—to make a dramatic improvement, in process time and people efficiency. Dr. Michael Hammer, the American process re-engineering specialist, has a very good definition:

"The radical redesign of business processes for dramatic improvement"

The first word is radical; RE-ENGINEERING gives us the opportunity to start with a clean sheet of paper. It gives you the chance to start afresh, to create a process that has low overheads, is fast, accurate, cheap, and easy to use (FACE).

The second word is dramatic, RE-ENGINEERING is not about a 5 percent change; it is about dramatic change where the new process is unlikely to have any resemblance to the existing process. This is where you can create real added value for your company.

The difficulty that HR personnel will experience is that of either being creative or innovative in their thinking. Most people in today's HR are still very conservative in their approach to change. RE-ENGINEERING requires a very bold and aggressive approach—which is often why consultants are used.

Use the FACE technique often, you will find this a big help, think how we can make this process: Faster, more Accurate, Cheaper, and Easier?

In the classic IBM finance study they were able to take a 6-day process run by four people and reduce it to 1 person taking 4 hours—that's both radical and dramatic. Also consider that the volume of business they were able to transact went up by a factor of 100.

Using your skills as discussed in step 3, redraw the new RE-ENGINEERING map. A tip here when doing this—do not look at your original ET map or you will just end up modifying it, getting a small improvement in performance.

As before, when you draw up this map put the same departments in the swim lanes, and in the same order. When you have finished your new map—put them both on the wall and you will see a real difference.

Stage 5—calculating the added value—RE-ENGINEERING is a massive contributor to creating added value. What needs to be taken into the equation?

Cost of old process $\times$ times used per year = (old process cost p.a.)

Cost of new process $\times$ times used per year = (new process cost p.a.)

(Old process cost p.a.) – (new process cost p.a.) = total value

Total value – Cost of the HR's work = Added value to the company p.a.

Practice exercise—Producing a business process map

Postal delivery process—M. Co. America—Stages 1–2

- Post received 7.30 am in post room.
- Post opened approximately 250 items per day.
- Two people are involved in this operation, which takes 30 minutes.
- All incoming items are recorded in a book—the book records the person who sent the correspondence, the company, the topic, and who it's been assigned to—one person does this task and it takes 1.5 hours.
- Difficult items are sent to a Senior Manager who will do the allocation—this can take some time and if this happens due to the delay, the item is normally put back into the system the next day for recording and then delivery.
- When the post-delivery clerk arrives he sorts the mail and loads the post trolley and commences the delivery of the mail. Sorting and loading takes about an hour.
- Delivery of the mail by the Post Delivery Clerk to the three offices. Calculate pushing the trolley from department to department; also calculate how long it takes to sign in the book for each item received.
- When the post clerk arrives back to the post room, someone later in the day, he checks the book to ensure all items of post have been signed for. If there are items where the recipient did not sign then the item is written in the book for delivery the next day, the postal clerk also writes a handwritten note explaining when the item was received, when it was attempted to be delivered.
- Don't forget—the post room staff work 8 hours a day. They will have a 1-hour lunch break, tea/coffee breaks (15 minutes).
- This process has been in operation for 10 years and everyone liked it.
- Try to complete stages 1 and 2 and draw up a process map—calculate ET.

The mapping process in action

Practice exercise—working out ET

Postal delivery process—M. Co. America—Stages 3–5

Be dramatic and radical—don't look at your old process map.

When you have finished calculate the value added and cost of this over a reasonable period—3 years.

In Conclusion

RE-ENGINEERING gives the HR department two significant advantages. First it removes things that take away performance from people—namely, out of date processes. Secondly and most important, if you are creating an added value HR function RE-ENGINEERING gives you the capability of creating large amounts of added value and at the same time getting a better business integration and acceptance at strategic level. Using your own process to start with, there is absolutely nothing to lose by trying this method—but everything to gain.

Getting results and creating value using this method is really effective—in early 2016 a company used this process and improved output by 50 percent —no extra staff were employed and the complete process end to end took less than 6 months. This is added value in action!

Case Study Re-engineering and Work Flow Management—Richards Engineering 2016

Richards is an engineering company founded in 1860 by Everard Richards, an engineer from Sheffield. The business went from father to son, and went public in 1991. The stock value had grown, very slowly and the city analysts viewed the shares as a safe but a low-income choice.

Richards's product was spherical joints used in the gear linkages of certain sports cars. Its market had always been in the UK, and its product sold through one distributor whom the company had worked with since 1860.

Richards had only one competitor in its market, Squires Engineering, who had come into the market in late 2009. Then in 2015, and it came as a complete surprise, Squires started selling the same product 8 percent cheaper than the Richards product. Quality appeared to be the same, and in the course of 9 months Richards had seen its market share evaporate, share value plummet, and things became serious.

Facts about the Company

Engineering (Operations) have taken delivery of high-speed robotic lathes valued at £2.5 million, which as yet have not been used. Some facts about the company and its structured and reward scheme.

- Richards employs 1,390 people, all based in one factory site.
- The top end structure consists of a managing director (Mr. Richards) and five main board directors, which are Support Services, Finance, Engineering Operations, Sales, and a Marketing Department. The key function is the Engineering operations that employ 1,143 people, which includes the Director. This leaves 245 employees in the remaining functions.
- Current production is 10,000 units per day.
- Profit is 9 percent over cost.
- Profit per unit is £50.00.
- All of the staff have been with the company for over 2 years.
- Mr. Richards has purchased five robotic lathes that can produce 2,000 units each in 8 hours. These are self-loading and completely automatic.
- Total SUC per person is £46.00.

Restrictions

- The Company is subject to international employment law.
- There is no possibility of significantly increasing the salary/remuneration budget.
- It is important that any proposals are introduced immediately.
- Mr. Richards is very much against making anyone redundant.
- Mr. Richards has little respect for HR and their associated services as he feels the only "bread winner" is operations engineering.

Please Note

The name and location of the company have been changed, as this is a real consultancy project.

The assignment briefing:

- Richards has just received an order, which requires them to produce 15,000 units a day—this will happen in 2 months time (this is from the start of the project).
- The consultancy project was to come out with a plan to make this happen—if necessary use the robotic lathes (but only at night).

What happened? Part 1

- Organizational chart produced.
- Concept of two, 8-hour night shifts agreed with three existing employees from production, working in attendance on each or the two night shifts.

The Process Explained

- Units of work established—production produce (current) 17 units a day per person.
- Packing pack 25.5 units per person a day.

What happened? Part 2

- 196 workers from production moved to packing to guarantee the manual ability to pack a total of 15,000 units a day

- 6 workers moved from packing to night shifts (robotic lathes)
- Lost production in production (202 people $\times$ 17 units) = 3,434
- Night production requirements 5,000 + 3,434 = 8,434 units
- Total units in 24 hours = 15,000 produced and packaged

Value created:

Profit per item £50 $\times$ 5,000 $\times$ 226 (number of working days per year = £56,500,000)

Cost involved:

Equipment	£2,500,000
Fees and workflow costs	£ 100,000
Total costs 2015 £250,000 + £100,000	= £2600,000

Calculation (This is the standard formula in HR for calculating added value)

Value – cost = added value in 1 year

£56,000,000 – £2,600,000 = £53,400,000

This example was featured in a television documentary with Dr Miller in 2016 on How to create value and improve productivity.

5.2   Refocus Recruitment

Why We Need to Improve

Google quote:

"let in one bozo and others will surely follow"—CEO Google

Without doubt attracting, interviewing, and retaining a talent is a critical issue. Despite millions of unemployed workers, there is still an acute shortage of talent. Although the amount of people that are applying for jobs is amazing, companies still feverishly search for the people who will make the difference between 10 and 20 percent annual growth in profit. Critical talent is scarce, and about to become scarcer because of two looming trends: the retirement of the babyboom generation and the growing international skills gap.

The weakest link as always is recruitment—no-one who has not been trained since 2014 should be allowed anywhere near an interviewing room regardless of their position in the company. Recruitment is the gateway into the company; any shortcuts or poor practice here will be very costly to sort out later on.

Cost reducing the cost of Recruitment is what many HR functions have focused on - IT'S FALSE ECONOMY. The more time and money you spend on recruitment, the better your recruitment will be, provided you follow a process approach which we will discuss later.

That the side of the equation that most organizations focus on. It's the wrong approach; the cost of recruitment is miniscule when compared to the cost of making a mistake. In many organizations it has been found that poor performers account for 22 percent of the workforce. Looking at the real cost of making a mistake is worth working out and showing others. Looking at an organization that employees 3,000 people:

ESUC £46 × Hours lost per day 7 × PWD 226 = £72,772.00 per year
Number of poor performers 660 ×
£72,772 × likely period of employment 20 years = £960,590,400.00

So it begs the questions why are recruiters made responsible for poor recruitment decisions? The figure is not complete, as you would have to add on all of the costs of training given to poor performers plus the extra management and supervision time they need. So in our overview on recruitment it's clear that the cost of doing the recruitment is not the area where we need to save money but the area where we should invest more.

The latest research is included in my book on recruitment (2017) but it shows that less recruitment mistakes are made if a process approach is adopted and adhered to by the entire organization and that all personnel involved in the process are trained.

Now if the person were a poor performer you would lose 35 hours a week nonproductive time—at your leisure you can work out the cost in 1 year.

New process, new results

In the recruitment process there are three key areas where instant improvement can be made.

The first is testing.

This should not be optional but essential for every interview at every level. In 2011 the Obarni case brought the horror of shoddy interviewing to the public notice. Obarni, a Nigerian, resident in Germany who professed to be a qualified doctor, was employed in the Health service in the UK. On his first day in the job he administered an overdose of a drug—killing the patient. He fled to Germany to avoid prosecution. Simple testing would have determined that Obarni was not a competent, qualified Medical Doctor.

An occupational test is simply a psychological test used in the world of work. There have been numerous attempts to define what a psychological test is. One definition for a test is:

> "a standardized sample of behavior which can be described by a numerical scale or category system." (Cronbach 1984)

Psychological or "psychometric" tests aim to maximize objectivity by standardizing test conditions, instructions, time, content, scoring, and interpretation.

The History of Testing

Psychological tests have been shown to be among our most powerful aids in the crucial problem of selecting, developing, and counseling people at work. Estimates by some researchers have shown for example that large increases in the GNP could result from more widespread use of tests in selection.

In Ancient China, the selection of civil servants was undertaken by written tests and required candidates to show verbal creativity by completing rhyming couplets. In the seventeenth century, Samuel Pepys, on becoming Clerk of the Acts of the King's Ships, introduced a test for the rank of lieutenant in the British Navy which he knew many rich but unmotivated young men would fail.

Although Binet in France in 1905 is usually credited with the world's first standardized individual test of mental ability for children, it was not until the outbreak of World War I that occupational tests were employed on any scale. The important part which tests played in the classification of vast numbers of people in both world wars led to much activity in the development of tests more suitably adapted to the needs of commerce and industry—an activity which continues to the present day.

Occupational tests are now used for all types and levels of job selection: from unskilled factory worker to senior management positions. Most of this usage tends to be in larger organizations, clearly because they employ more staff, but also because they have more readily appreciated the difficulties of obtaining comparable assessments from different interviewers.

Testing

There are all sorts of tests you can use. The skill of the professional interviewer is to use only reliable tests that are valid for the job in hand.

Testing materials are best purchased from reputable suppliers, some of which are as follows:

Saville and Holdsworth (SHL)
The Test Agency—Hogrefe Ltd
NEFFR Nelson
The Psychological Corporation

Testing has been around for many years. Psychometric tests enable you to ascertain WHAT THE CANDIDATE CAN DO NOW. You can then do a mathematical comparison with them against an industry or group average, known as a norm group. Thus, when you test you compare the results against a standard and appropriate norm group, rather than compare against the group you are testing. It provides you with an accurate measure at the point of testing. It therefore helps to reduce the risk of employment error.

The "tests" are normally paper and pencil, run in strict, exam conditions, and are always timed. Be careful of web-based tests—they may be very convenient—but unless you can see the candidate—you will have no idea of who has really completed the test.

Ability testing is normally for skills selection, for example, selection of correct components, assembly of parts from a selection. Typing tests/speed and accuracy tests also fall into this category. These are easy to design and can be very cost-effective.

Other tests may include physical testing for fitness or to detect an issue that may affect performance of the job such as eyesight, color blindness, hearing, and active listening skills.

The Second—Personality Profiling

These are not tests but questionnaires which help us understand someone's personality. There are thousands on the market—select with care as you get what you pay for. The reason why personality profiling is so important is that it enables you to select the right person for the job. People who are in occupations that fit well with their personality enjoy the work more and are normally more reliable and productive. So if you can match ability via testing and personality via profiling you have a much better chance of getting the right person in the right job and get a person who will perform well.

It's not by chance that companies who have been voted America's best places to work, spend a great deal of time and money on getting this right.

For recruitment, promotion, or development for supervisory level and below we would suggest the NEO or the EPI. This measures the Big Five personality factors:

- Neuroticism
- Extrovert
- Openness
- Agreeable
- Conscientiousness

The NEO is probably easier to use and is certainly quicker to score. Both are 60 questions and give a quick profile of the candidate.

For managers up to CEOs there is a wider but more confusing range, the top two are the SHL OPQ32 and the McRay&Coster NEO—PIR.

These are very accurate and provide the interviewer with sufficient information to base a recruitment decision on. They are also excellent tools for developing or selecting staff for promotion. Both have built-in lie detectors and consist of over 200 questions. There is a great temptation to use free profilers off of the web. Many of these as one of my clients found to his cost and embarrassment are written for a laugh and have no reliability or validity tests to back them up. My advice, if you want to be the best—use the best.

The Third —Prewritten and Scoreable Questions

Prewritten questions are essential for two main reasons:

They focus on the key criteria of the job and they are a major step in preventing interview bias. With increasing cases of litigation it is essential to firm up and bring up to date how we conduct the interview.

All the main questions (knowledge based and directly linked to the criteria) are scored out of 10. The scoring is done as the interview progresses. The knowledge-based questions are grouped together for each of the key criteria, with 4–6 questions for each criterion. The criteria selected are normally but not exclusively the key competencies for the job. When we speak to the candidate we signpost the criteria we are going to ask questions about and do this by setting the topic as a scene setter. Here is an example of how it works.

For the job of Senior Accounts Manager, this job has identified the following key criteria:

- Working with teams
- Current Accountancy Processes
- Working under pressure
- Strategic planning
- Supporting business unit managers

Working with teams

For each series of questions the prequestion sheet is completed with the appropriate knowledge-based questions written on it. This would be done at the time the advert is discussed.

Interviewer

Good Morning—this is Mr. Smythe—he is head of Finance and will be interviewing with me. We will be asking you a number of questions about your past experience. Please give short and concise answers to the questions; when we have finished the questions at the end of the interview, you will have the opportunity to ask us any questions that you have—is that OK?

Scene setter Working with Teams	Score
1. What experience have you had at managing teams in the past 5 years?	
2. Give me an example where you have dealt with conflict in a team	
3. From your experience, what is the optimum size for an effective team?	
4. Do you encourage competition between teams?	
Total Score	

Scene setter—"we will now ask you a series of questions on working with teams"

Q. 1. Interviewer

What experience have you had at managing teams in the past 5 years?

A. Interviewee—I have run a department of 50 people for the last 5 years.

Interviewer Probing question

Were they split into teams?

A. Interviewee
Yes by function, when I first took on the job it was just one department, but dividing the department into teams worked really well.

Interviewer—probing question

Whose idea was it?

Interviewee—mine

Interviewer—probing question What were the benefits?

A. Interviewee
We were better equipped to meet our deadlines, never missed any so far, and unauthorized absence stopped. Also, there is a much better working environment.

What experience have you had at managing teams in the past 5 years?	10	← Score

The second question on team working:

Q. 2 Interviewer

Give me an example where you have dealt with conflict in a team.

A. Interviewee—We had one employee who was very disruptive—always talking on his mobile phone and texting.

Probing question—How were you involved?

A. Some of the team complained about him to me, I then spoke to him on a one to one and pointed out this was not acceptable in our department.

Probing question—Did that resolve the issue?

A. Interviewee—No, he took no notice so I had to give him a verbal warning in accordance with our procedures—that brought an immediate stop to the problem. He was not happy but understood why I had to pursue the matter.

Give me an example where you have dealt with conflict in a team	8	← Score

Q. 3. Interviewer

From your experience, what is the optimum size for an effective team?

A. Interviewee: I don't understand the question

Interviewer: From your experience, what is the optimum size for an effective team?

Interviewee: Sorry, I don't understand.

Interviewer: Don't worry—let's move onto the next question

From your experience, what is the optimum size for an effective team?	0	← Score

Q. 4. Interviewer

> Do you encourage competition between teams?

A. Interviewee—Yes it's a good thing provided it's well controlled. This is particularly the case when we do end of year accounts and we have a special payment system for the best teams. We get good results and the teams all like a bit of competition. Last year the winning team brought cakes for all the rest, which was really appreciated, also the end of year accounts was completed two days ahead of schedule, so the CFO was very happy.

Do you encourage competition between teams?	10	⬅ Score

Interviewer

> Scene setter – the next series of questions are about current accounting processes

New approach—new results. A process approach to effective recruitment

If you were to ask ten of your managers "what's the best way to interview," I suspect you would get ten different answers, each convinced that their way was the best. A look through LinkedIn shows what a vast range of different ideas there are on what should be done, ranging from the quest to make recruitment as cheap as possible to outlandish ideas that defy belief.

Every time you recruit you have the opportunity to make a decision—either good or bad. You can recruit talented people, average people, or people who are and are likely always to be poor performers. The financial crunch between 2012 and 2014 has shown all of us that most organizations were overstaffed; reductions in organizational numbers in many cases resulted in higher productivity and greater organizational efficiency. The reason that numbers could and have been reduced is that those companies had a disproportionate amount of poor and average performers—and yes someone had recruited them.

A survey completed in 2014 in the Middle East of over 1,000 employees in 110 large companies showed that talented people do almost 6 times more work than poor performers; the financial implications of inadequate recruitment are massive.

The traditional face-to-face interview

The reasons that just face-to-face recruitment fails are a combination of the following. This is not an opinion but based on reliable current studies and fact.

- Validity
  The unreliability of the face-to-face interview due to bias and the fact they do not measure what they are designed to do.
- Interviewer motivation
  Because interviews are a long process attentions spans wane. Accuracy of the interview is based on the interviewer's ability to pick the right applicant. If testing is omitted this becomes an unreliable method.
- Office politics
  Office politics can result in a significant blow to interview validity. Interviews are relatively easy to "fix" due to interviewers favoring certain candidates; they can nod and smile to encourage those they like, while provoking unfavorable applicants with negative or blunt remarks. This can mean the interview acts as a stage for office politics and power networking, with members of the interview board lobbying inferior candidates because they match their interests (Bozionelos, 2005). Woodzicka and LaFrance (2005) also demonstrated that interviewers who ask mildly sexually harassing questions to female interviewees cause dramatic drops in interview performance; the candidates spoke less fluently, gave lower quality answers, and asked less job-related questions.
- Lack of training
  The vast majority of people who interview have been inadequately trained, or not trained at all. The results are apparent as interviewers do not tell candidates what dimensions will be covered/assessed in the interviews as this will cause applicants to prepare answers that say the right thing/what interviewers want to hear. Klehe et al. (2008) found that transparency greatly increased the construct-validity of the interview dimensions; when applicants were able to prepare, their answers better reflected what the questions were actually asking. Furthermore, the increase in

content validity meant that the strengths and weaknesses between applicants were more easily distinguishable, as answers were no longer incomparable due to the vague/invalid nature of interview questions.

- Unstructured interviews

  An unstructured interview with potential future employees is a method used by managers in order to "read between the lines," size them up, and ascertain whether or not they are the right person for the position. Managers have a heavy preference for unstructured interviews because it allows them to go with their gut and use their intuition, potentially spotting idiosyncrasies that would be missed in analytical measures. Managers commonly overestimate the influence of intuition, while dramatically underestimating the validity of more robust measures (i.e., paper-and-pencil tests, structured interviews, etc.) in "X-factor"/"right stuff" thinking for finding talented employees.

- Myers (2002) "interview illusion"—an unstructured, intuition-based interview may focus more on a candidate's declared intentions and future behavior, but these are likely to be a less useful predictor than their past performance.

- Lievens, Highhouse, and De Corte (2005) —managers placed more emphasis on competencies assessed by unstructured interviews than competencies measured by tests, irrespective of what the competency was.

- Managers emphasized the importance of Extraversion over general mental ability when the former was ascertained through unstructured interview while the latter was found through pencil-and-paper test. Yet, managers preferred general mental ability when found through unstructured interview than Extraversion when decided by tests. Therefore, this is evidence that managers rely heavily on their instincts when sizing up an individual.

The Panel Interview

One of the most potentially ineffective ways of interviewing, yet many organizations still use it. The reason they do is to avoid accountability, to be seen to be involved and in some instances people are on the panel so they can show their peers how clever they are.

Candidates often find the panel interview overwhelming and intimidating and for that reason introverts do not perform well in such conditions. The most effective would be two people interviewing, the line manager together with the interviewing professional. Secondary interviews should also be avoided, as this is normally a sign that no one wants accountability for the final decision-making.

The Process Approach

A process approach helps to avoid most of our problem areas and also the underlying issue that managers, in the main, only recruit people they like. That "like" is often made up of the most amazing preconceived ideas that would not survive any sort of rational audit. The process approach is a way of having a standardized format across the organization and ensuring a conformance to standards.

The process approach may need to be modified to fit individual organizational needs and that is your choice.

The process consists of nine sequential steps—each very important to the total objective of recruiting great people.

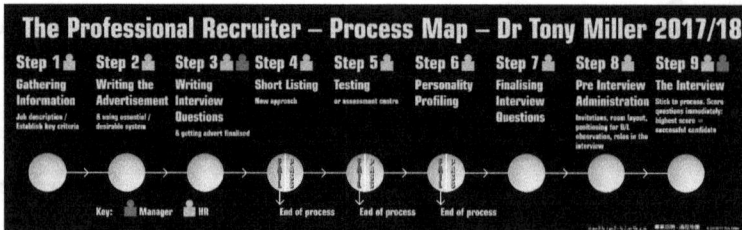

The end-to-end process is backed by a massive amount of research and is currently thought to be the best way of getting high-caliber employees (talent); the process is fully explained in detail in the book on recruitment published in 2017 by Dr Tony Miller.

As a business partner you do need to be a master of your own processes and be able to work with and show the business how your processes really add value.

5.3   Performance Appraisal

What Are the Benefits of Appraisal?

Ask any professional HR manager about the benefits of performance appraisal and you will hear all the normal attributes—good development tool, essential to determine training requirements, key tool for motivation, ideal for gathering data, for setting performance objectives, for measuring employee competence, tool to justify bonus and rewards, etc.

The final comment is normally that it is best practice.

Yet ask the same question of a senior line manager and the response is normally very different.

The majority of managers seem to have the view that appraisal time does not justify the end result. This is a conflict of opinions so who is responsible for the output and added value of the appraisal system?

Who Has Responsibility for the Performance Appraisal?

If you decouple measurable output from performance appraisal, then most HR professionals put their hands up to owning the process.

However, once the term measurement output is mentioned, then the responsibility for the process and the output seems to transfer quickly to line management.

With performance appraisal being the single biggest tool for objective setting and performance measurement, how can it degenerate so quickly into an organizational orphan?

In the vast number of performance appraisal systems that are in place it's inconceivable that so much can be spent on a process that delivers so little yet is still viewed as best HR practice.

This is due to a common myth that best practice must always produce best practice results. If it is best HR practice then perhaps any HR bonus should be calculated on added value measurable output from the system.

As the process is clearly a shared responsibility with the line management, the output must form the basis of a shared key performance indicator.

Before you sign up to this being a good idea, you need to read on and see what is involved to get benefit from this system.

Serious Defect in Most Appraisal Systems

The operating fault of most current systems lies not just with the process and lack of accountability for bottom line results but with a far simpler issue, an issue that is cheap, quick, and easy to remedy.

After speaking with over 1,000 HR professionals worldwide from a wide spectrum of industries, it is evident that in the majority of cases the focus of appraisal makes positive measurable outcomes impossible.

The consensus of opinion seems to be that once the appraisal system is installed, after the first year a pattern of how the appraisal actually runs becomes evident. The actual time spent doing the appraisal seems to vary to within plus or minus 15 minutes, the mean tending to be one hour in duration. What is of great interest is how that time is used.

It seems that the majority of the appraisal time is spent reviewing the previous year. In fact the figure quoted amounts to a massive 80 percent. That's 80 percent looking back: on performance against objectives, identifying training needs, and other factors that should not be discussed at a performance appraisal. We term this the rearview mirror effect.

The fault with this approach is that nothing can be done about the past or past performance—what's past is history, nothing will change what's already happened.

The only thing managers can plan for and be successful with is the future. This obsession with the previous year's past performance and activities is the single biggest reason for appraisals failing.

The rearview mirror approach is not compatible with today's fast-moving dynamic business approach.

With such a strong "past" focus it leaves only 20 percent of the time of the appraisal left for future focus. It's not surprising that objectives are poorly set and little, if any, real measurement of performance is planned or takes place. Because of this managers are unwittingly setting their staff up for ongoing failure.

This effect of setting employees up to fail is very real and costly. Training is then identified based on failure or weaknesses.

When the employee fails, the feeling of failure, or of a job not well done, pushes motivation down and hangs like a shadow of doom till the next appraisal, so training (normally the cure-all solution) is prescribed based on a failure which happened probably 9 months before the appraisal.

Training then identified at appraisal goes through the system and it can be 6 months before it takes place.

To recap, in this example a total of 15 months elapsed time has been taken to rectify a past mistake or shortfall and provide a solution, in this case, training. This retrospective approach to appraisal makes no business sense and could easily be avoided by taking a different approach. HR managers, line managers, and certainly managing directors seem to be unaware of the true cost of an appraisal system.

The Real Cost of Appraisal Formula 6

If appraisal is the most important goal-setting tool an organization has, then we must be confident that it will yield good returns on investment and add value. So let's examine the cost of appraisal for a company employing 5,000 people with an average employee unit cost of £46.00 per hour.

For each appraisal

Appraiser's time preparing 0.5 hours × £46	£23.00
Appraisee's time preparing 0.5 hours × £46	£23.00
Appraisal time for appraiser 1 × £46	£46.00
Appraisal time appraise 1 × £46	£46.00
After the appraisal—completing documentation appraise 0.5 hours × £46	£23.00
After the appraisal—talking and reflecting appraise 0.5 hours × £46	£23.00
HR processing time for each appraisal 0.5 hours × £46	£23.00
Subtotal	£207.00
3,000 employees × £207	£621,000.00

In addition it would be fair to add the cost of misdirected training identified from appraisal. This could be as high as 70 percent of the training budget—the cost of which would need to be added to the calculation.

In our example we have a cost to the business of £621,000—to get just a simple return on investment we need to get each year £621,000 of measurable bottom line benefits. Can your appraisal system deliver this type of performance?

If you go beyond return on investment to seek added value then it would be reasonable to expect to see a 20 percent added value each year. In other words each year the system is in place we should expect to see minimum measurable benefits of £745,200. Can your system deliver this type of business performance?

What Needs to Change to Produce Real Advantage from Performance Appraisal?

Producing real results from appraisal, whether it is development, competency improvement, or business performance, is achievable simply by changing the focus and emphasis of any traditional appraisal.

The only thought any manager should have at appraisal is "How can I set this person up to be successful?" With that thought clearly in mind, the rest should be straightforward.

Time reviewing the past (which we cannot change) should be reduced to 20 percent of the appraisal time—looking forward, setting SMART or WWW objectives, and discussing success should be our prime and only focus. At least 80 percent of focused attention must be for success in the future.

If, for any objective, there is any genuine reason that the employee (appraise) cannot meet the objective through lack of skill, knowledge, or experience, then some form of action, perhaps training, needs to be arranged prior to the objective start date.

This is a critical action if our employee is to be successful—training first before objective.

New focus = new results.

Once objectives have been set and agreed, the measurement of results must be an ongoing, a regular, and scheduled activity—after all, is this not the basis of why we employ managers? This must take the form of an ongoing and performance-focused interaction between appraise and appraiser.

The focus on everyone being successful should be the manager's overriding aim. This is not easy with difficult and challenging employees, the lazy, and the unliked. A good manager should apply the same approach to everyone—change will happen only when trust and credibility have been established.

Is Appraisal a Motivational Tool?

Is appraisal a motivational tool? Just ask yourself, will employees be more motivated by failure—the old rear mirror approach; or will employees be more motivated by success in an environment that breeds success; the forward success-driven approach.

Motivational success through appraisal can be measured. Do some statistical analysis such as measuring sickness levels before the new approach and then examining the sickness levels after. Also, look at staff turnover both before the new system and then after. Staff satisfaction surveys are also a useful indicator.

Where does 360-degree appraisal fit with the new model?

The 360-degree appraisal is yet another shining example of what is believed to be best practice.

Does it work?

How much does it cost to run the process?

What's the level of return on investment, and, when calculated, what will be an acceptable added value return on the process?

This type of appraisal is very expensive, not only in time and administration but also in lost productivity.

Most advocates of this process will say it's a great motivational tool and that because it's so open it is beneficial to all.

If this is the case, then providing the added value will be easy and should be carried out each year—but I suspect it is not.

Just do the calculation for yourself based on our example and see how much extra is needed just to cover the cost.

You can then make your own judgment on whether or not you think it is right for your organization. The term motivation is often wrapped in with the benefits of appraisal. If appraisal is a key motivational tool then managers need help.

If you must use 360-degree appraisal—then at least use one that works such as: one operated by Bill Best, a chartered Psychologist

Managers Need Help

Performance against agreed targets needs to be measured and discussed throughout the year, with success celebrated as appropriate. Then, when the next round of appraisals starts, the majority of employees will be confident in the knowledge that you're focusing on making them successful. Success breeds success.

Most managers have difficulty with setting measurable performance targets. Although this is a key part of the job it is seldom tackled with much enthusiasm. Short workshops on setting specific objectives are a good way to start, using the SMART process to help them to focus.

Another good investment would be a briefing on the value of coaching and using Management By Walking About and it is a good tool to keep ongoing involvement in place.

A key input factor for managers and supervisors' bonuses should be based on the percentage performance achieved during the year.

By linking directly to pay the incentive is created to make things happen.

Organizational Benefits

Changing the focus for appraisal really is a case of everything to gain and little to lose. Before changing anything gather base data on what exists now, if any.

Try to compile figures, which will show exactly the cost of appraisal and what if any quantifiable performance improvements there are.

This base information is needed for when you start to produce added value charts later.

Some of the organizational benefits that should be seen include: projects delivered on time and within budget, reduced absenteeism levels, improved staff morale, reduced training budget, a more agile organization, and lower staff turnover in the long term.

The process will clearly identify poor performing managers, supervisors, and employees and will enable a definite and measurable impact on the bottom line to be seen.

Although this might only seem appropriate to the private sector, many of the benefits mentioned do map very nicely into the public sector.

There should also be a change in the way HR is viewed, as this gives a clear indicator that HR is adding value by using business skills to enhance business performance.

Individual Benefits

Connectivity has become an issue in the UK, with a number of surveys showing that staff increasingly has low connectivity with their employers.

As the new appraisal focus is based on a shared responsibility for success, there will be a greater feeling of inclusion and the possibility for building long-term connectivity.

Rewards based on measurable performance are also fair and equitable and will be seen as such.

Those showing potential through improved performance will be the first candidates for development, while training takes on a new and specific role, which is directly linked to achieving business objectives, a prerequisite for IIP. Training, in whatever form, will also be seen as a key tool for individual success.

Finally, there will be an overall view that we are doing the right thing and something that is worth doing—because it's measurable and taken seriously.

5.4   Motivation and Its Relationship with Pay and Rewards

Before you reel at the thought of pay being the only motivator—it's not. The way we treat and manage employees is by far the greatest individual motivator. Time after time on published surveys, the top companies who people prefer to work for are not the best payers. In fact, on reading the last survey on principally American companies, most of the top ten were not that well known and were certainly not high payers.

Changing any existing bonus scheme will prove to be one of the most difficult but potentially rewarding activities you can perform. Why? Because it's fair and it produces massive added value.

First we need to believe in the old saying "One shoe does not fit all." This certainly applies to any type of real bonus scheme.

First who should be entitled to bonus? Going back to our concept of differentiation described earlier we have three groups within any organization.

The poor performers—they don't qualify for any bonus payments, increments, or any sort of enhancements.

The average performers—well, this group do the minimum to stay employed, so why would you want to pay any of this group bonus, perhaps cost of living awards, but that's it.

Finally our last group our talented group, our high performers, not to be confused with high potential. This group according to Jack Welsh (former CEO General Electric) and the late Steve Jobs (Apple) do almost 50 percent more than average workers. This is the only group that should be on the bonus radar. We can afford to pay this group huge bonuses. Why? Because they are worth it and it's the group we don't want to leave. It is this group that are the future and the lifeblood of any successful organization.

By paying the talented group big bonuses this will inspire those who are average performers to try harder and join the talented group, thus pulling up the standard of the organization. From a manpower planning point of view:

More talented people = less total employees

This is due entirely to the amount of work done, so there is a double benefit. Showing the added value of this policy is easy to do and it just involves calculating.

The value of the extra productivity plus less turnover of talented people plus productivity improvement of any average or poor performers who are replaced minus the cost of extra bonus paid.

However, the talented group must, individually, earn their bonus and as such this will give rise to healthy competition. This approach works in public and private sectors and is not linked to success, which is entirely due to international market changes.

If you are considering moving in this direction—do so with care. The people who will complain the most, the people who will talk about strike action are—the poor performers.

When designing a good bonus system, do so from the end point; what is it you are trying to achieve? There are three parts to think about:

Setting the tasks or objectives—these need to be done to insure that the potential bonus is specifically aligned with strategic objectives, they need to be allocated points so that the total objectives are measured out of a 100 percent. This makes scoring at a later date much easier. There is a tool that helps with this—known as strategic action plans.

Is the task/objectives team or individual based? If team based then a hopper bonus-type approach would be appropriate.

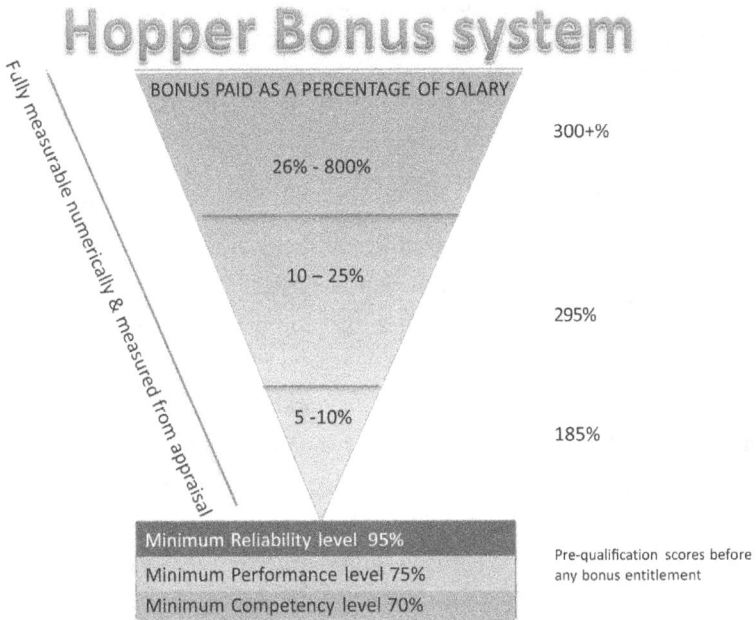

The task/objective with this scheme you need to set very clear competency standards that must be achieved by the entire team (this takes care of quality) and also the minimum performance standard to be achieved by the entire team, before anyone can get bonus. Once the competence and performance have been achieved it is all systems go for earning some serious bonus and creating real productivity. What about the outstanding individual?

Individuals—Outstanding individuals need to be recognized. Once this system is set up it's easy to work out whom the high performers are and to give them an extra payment. This needs to be over and above any team bonus. If individuals are not part of a team then clear objective setting still needs to be in place and so too the scoring method. Bonus can then be allocated based on actual scores as a percentage of salary.

By taking this approach we have satisfied all the needs of the Adair model for creating high performance. But what about the managers?

Managers' bonuses should be based on the performance of their teams compared to the performance of other managers' teams. If the manager creates, motivates, and produces teams that can outperform other teams then they can go on to a ladder bonus system which is purely productivity based. Good managers will earn a lot and poor managers about the same as the people they manage.

Other Considerations

There are many other ways to motivate employees—this is the job of the line management. One suggestion you might want to consider is the use of power briefings. This has been used to great effect in the finance industry and with production companies in China. At the start of the working week at exactly the start of the working day the manager/leader has a power briefing for 4–5 minutes. During this briefing, which is completely focused on the current week, what's critical to make the week a success is discussed. This is a great aid in getting employees focused for the week and to start fully informed about what's critical. This is not a forum for discussing the previous week's activities nor is it a general gossip forum.

The giving of "Goodies" for rewarding outstanding effort. Some companies have used this to good effect. In one company the "Gift" of a Land cruiser was offered and given to the manager who could reduce sickness levels by the largest percentage. As before, the value was the cost of the lost day minus the cost of the Land cruiser. Another added value costable activity by New HR.

Please remember it's not New HR's job to take over the role of motivation, but it is our responsibility to provide managers with the tools and processes that will maximize our human capital.

5.5   Training

Training accounts not only for a significant part of the HR budget, but also attached to each training day is the ESUC of the employee who is attending the course.

Training costs (see training budget Excel download) comprises of four unit costs:

- Cost of In-House training with an In-House Trainer
- Cost of In-House training with an external Trainer
- Cost of External training
- Cost of Education (courses that provide an internationally recognized qualification)

In addition is the ESUC cost per person attending the course—so the total cost is a combination of these two factors.

So How Do We Prove Training Adds Value?

Most training carried out by organizations is competency-based training. We devote on average 95 percent of our training budget on making sure this happens. If you take a hard look at this we are making sure that our employees are competent to do the job we are paying them for. This should guarantee the organization:

- Safety (people are doing the right things in the right standardized way)
- Conformance to standards (people are following the processes, rules, and required regulations in the organization)
- Quality assurance. If the two items above are in place then you have a degree of confidence that your quality standards will be met.

From an added value point of view these essential stills carry with them very little in terms of real measured added value. Nobody in the organization, for example, will get excited if your training improves Mr. Chan's competency score from 65 to 70 percent. If you were to calculate this value, the response would be it's not real value as they are being paid to be competent anyway. So the good news is don't bother evaluating competency training improvements. It's a line manager's responsibility and they will come up with the new scores normally at performance appraisal time. A word of caution—your training budget is based mainly on competence requirements so you have to make sure it's done.

The next area is of greater importance if you are looking to produce value added. These courses will and must produce measurable added value and as such need to be properly evaluated. We use the 10-step model to do this.

The number of courses and the types of training that produce measurable bottom line results are very few. Groups of professional training managers struggle to get a list of over five such programs. Remember the courses are not competency based, so see if you can add to their short list.

- Delivering project ahead of schedule and under budget
- Renegotiating existing contracts
- New business process re-engineering
- Predictive manpower planning and forecasting
- Delivering budgets under agreed spend
- Train the trainer programs
- Using innovative techniques to reduce operating cost
- Using NLP to improve sales and marketing
- Applying company rules to reduce lost hours
- Organizational rightsizing techniques

As you can see, the list is quite small but the value added is massive. Other courses you may expect to see are team working and new leadership skill. Although they will produce added value they must be done in conjunction with organizational change. The first time it is done it would be added value—thereafter it would be absorbed as a competence.

Training has a positive effect on employees. Regular training keeps employees mentally engaged and evidence shows that good training has a direct positive impact on reducing sickness and cementing loyalty.

This case study on using added value training and measuring shows the 10-step model in operation. Although only a small piece to training, just look at the added value created in 1 year.

An Area Health Authority
Case study

Step 1 Business Need

In a meeting with the Senior Administrator it was clear that savings needed to be made.

Examination of what needed to happen seemed to focus on the need to improve the value for money spends that the authority made. In other words, on all external contracts were they getting the best deal? The Senior Administrator thought that for other areas of the business and their operation every possible economy had been made.

Step 2 Analyses

An examination of purchasing procedures showed that within the Administration area a number of senior people were involved with significant contracts. Further examination showed that none had received training on the methodologies of purchasing and the only benchmark for success was accepting the lowest tender.

It was also evident that little effort was made to negotiate price other than regular statements that "we expect the best deal."

In total six members of staff were involved. Typical contract prices varied from £3,000 to £400,000.

Step 3 Design

Discussions within the training unit focused on providing a solution that could improve on contract success from strictly a price point of view. In other words, reduce the cost of individual contracts or item cost. There were a number of existing contracts that were either about to be negotiated or that could be renegotiated.

Current contract value was £706,000 and it was thought that training on specific negotiating skills would have at least a 10 percent improvement on current contracts in 1 year. The training on negotiating skills was to be incorporated in a management development program that was currently running and provided by an external supplier.

Step 4 Agreement

The agreement with the business was to provide Negotiation Skills training and to seek a "Pay back" on 10 percent on existing contracts to the value of £70,000.

Clearly there would be additional costs with the Management Training course, as it had to incorporate Negotiation Skills into its program

The business sponsor wanted the cost of the Management training in total, to be paid only if the benefits of the negotiation skills were realized.

The agreement therefore was between the three parties:

The business sponsor

The training department

The external supplier

The external supplier was to be paid once the results of the negotiation skills course were known

External supplier costs	£40,000 including negotiation skills
Benefits sought	£70,000 through renegotiation ofcontracts skills
Method of evaluation	each course member to produce hard evidence of each saving negotiated. The agreed figures to be approved by the Senior Administrator. The external provider to be paid when the evidence is available which should be within two months of the training

The training was performance based, as it would add value in 1 year.

Step 5 Delivery

Training carried out as designed with specific output requirements. Each course member was briefed on the need to evaluate the results of their negotiating skills and get the required sign off. During the course the trainer went through each trainee's individual negotiating or contract arrangements to provide as much help as necessary. Individual action plans were drawn up and agreed.

Steps 6,7,8 Validation Not Appropriate

Step 9 Evaluate

Evaluation of the results was as follows:

Course participant	Savings
a	£3,000
b	£172,500
c	?
d	£3,750
e	£500,000
f	£40,000
TOTAL IMPROVEMENT VALUE	£719,250
Less the cost of external training provider	£40,000
Less the cost of training departments involvement	
For consultancy, administration, and evaluation	£1,000
Actual benefit	£678,250

The evaluation results exceeded expectations by all concerned; all of the results were verified by the Sponsoring Manager and signed off.

Step 10 Feedback

Feedback of the results were given to:

> The sponsor
> The trainees
> Internal training department
> The external training provider

Training can be a massive contributor for added value. All that needs to change is getting a tighter focus on training that adds value. In instances where this has been used, training functions move swiftly into becoming profit centers. Consider running more added value courses and fewer competency-based courses, you can then use the value created to offset other training costs and aid in making the organizations training much cheaper by running with smaller budgets. Without any doubt all organizations react favorably where training can be shown to financially contribute to the organization.

Software sample downloads are provided by Duncan Williamson.

He is a specialist software designer and is available to work with you to customize your spreadsheet models. He has extensive experience in providing software solutions and customization ranges from small retail outlets to complex chemical processing organizations. Contact by e-mail HRanalytics@duncanwil.co.ukBill Best is a Charted Psychologist specializing in executive coaching and assessment centers. He has many years experience with 360-degree appraisal systems. Email: bill@ecp-360.com

CHAPTER 6

Trends and Correlations

6.1 Trends and Correlations

Trends give us time to plan and time to advice and alert other areas of the business. Failure to do this by workforce planners often has serious consequences in terms of panic recruitment and instability through competency drop. In this chapter we will look at some of the formulas that work and give examples of how they may be used, using some current case studies. Beware in the area of trend analysis as most of the old academic formulas either don't work well in practice or have been replaced with relevant software.

Some of the trends you would constantly review are:

- Age
- Sickness
- Competence (see productivity dashboard image under 2.10)
- Performance (see productivity dashboard image under 2.10)
- Reliability (see productivity dashboard image under 2.10)
- Predictable turnover
- Turnover
- Staff satisfaction
- Productivity
- Workforce requirement

All of the time trends can be plotted using Excel. Excel is also a great base for using other software such as Monte Carlo-type simulators for predictive forecasting and where comparable trends are compared using a correlation formula and other associated workforce planning software.

6.2   Turnover Trends

Introduction

> It is very important to get to grips with why we use turnover trends and what management information we are to deliver. It may be of use to know how many people leave the organization in a year—what's more important is to be able to spot trends and act on them to ensure the organization has the right amount of human resource at any given time and in every circumstance.

A) As far as turnover (often referred to as wastage) is concerned we have two completely different factors. Predictable turnover, for example, when people will retire or where we have people on long-term sickness and we will retire them. This information is known and predictable.

B) What is of greater interest is the stability of the organization and the effect on the organization of random turnover, that is, people leaving for whatever reason. It is this information that provides us with critical management information. Using predictive techniques we can then forecast likely trends in our organization.

Using both sets of information we can then fairly accurately know in each future year, how many people we will need to recruit, in what department, and what specialty skills are needed.

A) The labor turnover index

This index is basically the number of leavers expressed as a percentage of average employees. It is also known as the "crude" turnover (or wastage) index. However, in certain circumstances it can be quite a meaningless statistic and very misleading if given to managers to make decisions.

The simplest measure involves calculating the number of leavers in a period (usually a year) as a percentage of the number employed during the same period. This is known as the "crude wastage rate" and is calculated as follows:

$$\frac{\text{Number of leavers}}{\text{Average number employed}} \times 100$$

For example, if a business has 150 leavers during the year and, on average, it employed 2,000 people during the year, the labor turnover figure would be 7.5 percent:

$$\frac{150 \times 100}{2.000} = LTI\ 7.5\%$$

The importance of this to workforce planning is that what is needed is a measure that can predict future wastage and take into account both staying and leaving characteristics.

In an effort to provide a prediction of wastage for use with manpower planning, the labor turnover index, being so unstable and reflecting changes in length of service, may be little short of useless.

Also statistically it's not a good idea to include any employees who have been with the company for less than a year. This first year reflects poor recruitment, where employees don't like the job or where the employee finds the job not living up to their expectations and leaves. Also this first-year period includes the probationary period—where low scoring on competence, productivity, or reliability results in dismissal.

Although the labor turnover index (LTI) has been criticized quite heavily, in its defense it is easy to compute, and given a stable labor force, (may) be useful—advice here—forget it.

6.3 The Modified Labor Stability Index (Formula 3)

What is the purpose of this formula? This information is vital to management (not managers) on the stability of the organization's Human Capital. Here we are looking for potential trends, which may affect the business stability.

To overcome the problems with the LTI, the Labour Stability Index (LSI) was designed. This gives you a much better idea of what's going on in real business terms, particularly in turbulent times.

When using this index remove all of the employees that have less than one year's service to give a statistically more reliable picture. Also all predictable leavers should be removed (people who in that period will retire and long-term sickness leavers in the same yearly period).

$$\frac{\text{Total employed with more than one year's service now} - \text{(retirees and long-term sickness) in this period} \times 100}{\text{Total employed one year ago} - \text{(retirees and long-term sickness leavers) in this period}} = \text{LSI}$$

$$\frac{3,000 - (30 + 6) \times 100}{3,000 - (20 + 10)} = \text{LSI } 93.50\%$$

6.4   Cohort Analysis Formula 4

Cohort analysis requires following the "rate of survival" of a group (cohort) of employees through time. An example would be a large graduate recruitment program.

The following example shows the cohort analysis and from that you can plot the resulting survival curve, which shows the percentage of employees surviving (and remaining) at different points in time.

In statistical practice this is answered by a goodness-of-fit test which is concerned with whether the observed deviations from the fitted curve are such as could be accounted for by chance. In our view this is not usually the question of practical importance.

We really need to know whether the use of the fitted distribution will be sufficiently accurate for practical purposes and this can only be decided in the context of the problem in hand. It can well happen, for example, that a fit which would be rejected by a formal test of significance leads to predictions of sufficient accuracy for a particular purpose.

However, we regard this not as an argument for disregarding goodness-of-fit altogether but for interpreting the results sensibly, with due regard for the uses to which the analysis is to be put.

If a graphical method has been used, a good deal can be learnt from an inspection of the plot.

If the points show a marked departure from linearity as in the exponential fit one would clearly be very wary of using the fitted distribution for any purpose, which depended on extrapolating the line.

If, on the other hand, the points were linear but subject to a wide scatter about the line we would suspect that the form of the distribution fitted was satisfactory but that its parameters could not be determined very precisely.

The extent of the scatter would also give us some indication of the error of estimates of the survivor function made by reading off values from the line.

Predicting turnover (wastage)

> The easy way is to use the modified LSI formula, which will have excluded natural wastage (retirements) and long-term sickness, both of which are predictable. It then uses current turnover (wastage) data and simply uses a Monte Carlo-type simulator to project the predictable turnover for the next 3 years realistically, which is about as far ahead as is safe.

6.5   Use of Correlations (Formula 1)

The correlation or comparing of similar types of data allows us predictively to see what evidence exists to make future decisions. For example, in industry X do employees who receive a lot of training outperform those who have little or no training?

Doing a correlation would give us the answer and at the same time would enable us to make a sound decision on either, more or less investment in training, depending on the result.

Using the evidence of correlations stops us making judgments on what we feel or it's a good idea and allows us to act professionally based on the facts.

The list is endless, your role will be to decide what is of value to your organization and relevant.

Some examples:

Smokers—sickness

Performance appraisal scores—productivity on the job

Performance—age

Age group—sickness Competence—personality type

Productivity—sex

Competence—personality type

Duration with the company—reliability

Time with company—promotion level

There are three principal correlation formulas:

- Pearson's Moment Correlation formula
- Spearman's Correlation formula
- Kendall's W formula

In workforce planning we tend to use Pearson's formula 99.9 percent of the time. The formula can be worked out long hand—but I can't imagine why you would want to do this except that you can show off your prowess in mathematics. There are many software packages available such as analyze it (www.analyse-it.com/products/standard/correlation.aspx).

These correlation packages sit in Microsoft Excel and simply take the data and import it into the package and produce the r score.

The correlation or fit of the data is shown as its closeness to 1. So scores from 0.65 up to 1 would show the strength of the correlation. Below 0.65 there is no relationship worth considering. Correlations can be either positive or negative, the strength is still of importance.

Looking at the formula we can have a go at working out an example from data gathered from a consultancy project in Western America.

$$r = \frac{\sum XY - \frac{(\sum X)*(\sum Y)}{N}}{\sqrt{\left[\sum X^2 - \frac{(\sum X)^2}{N}\right]*\left[\sum Y^2 - \frac{(\sum Y)^2}{N}\right]}}$$

The issue we have been asked to solve is when new employees are tested they are given both Maths and Science test papers; the company concerned wants to know if there is a relationship between these tests.

If so, can one of the tests be dropped, this would save an estimated $750,000 p.a.

The sample size was over 1,500—in this example it has been reduced purely to give you an example and encourage you to have a go.

N = the number in the sample
X = The Maths score (range 0–20)
Y = The Science score (range 0–20)

Example 1: Data

Student:	Math (X):	Science (Y):	X2	Y2	X*Y
A	11	11	$11^2 =$	$11^2 =$	=
B	13	10	$13^2 =$	$10^2 =$	=
C	18	17	$18^2 =$	$17^2 =$	=
D	12	13	$12^2 =$	$13^2 =$	=
E	16	14	$16^2 =$	$14^2 =$	=
N =	ΣX =	ΣY =	ΣX2 =	ΣY2 =	ΣXY =

Have a go and see if you can do it!

EXAMPLE 1: EQUATION

$$r = \frac{\sum XY - \dfrac{(\sum X)*(\sum Y)}{N}}{\sqrt{\left[\sum X^2 - \dfrac{(\sum X)^2}{N}\right]*\left[\sum Y^2 - \dfrac{(\sum Y)^2}{N}\right]}}$$

Put in the numbers.

Finish the calculation

ANSWER: r =

In other words, there is a strong positive correlation between marks in maths and science. So what's the added value comment?

In this instance there is no need to do both tests—thus saving $750,000 p.a.

Answers available in Appendix 1 This chart was presented to the senior management team showing the progress that fresh graduates will make in the company. When challenged on the figures the gentleman concerned admitted, "I made them up" but was convinced, based on no empirical data that that was going to happen!

Average Competency
(Total Comp/Employees)

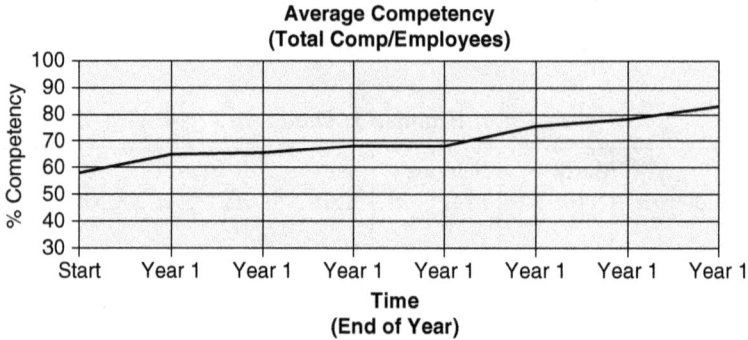

Don't make up data
Large Oil Company

6.6   Concepts of Forecasting

The old Manpower planning functions were masters at telling managers what they already were aware of—in other words they were flooded with retrospective information. This data unprocessed has very little if any use at all, but consumes management time in trying to understand it. We now have very good predictive software and it's that significant difference that will help us to transform retrospective data to meaningful and valuable information that will aid efficiency, give competitive edge, and also improve organizational efficiency.

Good news for workforce planners—you will (somewhere) have most of the data you need to do predictive forecasting. The bad news, some of it may not be statistically sound. For use either in correlations or in predictive techniques collected data need to be provided on a 1 to 100 scale. Many so-called Performance appraisal systems have a four-box category for marking, given titles such as Unsatisfactory, Satisfactory, Good, and Outstanding. Data collected in this way is statistically dead in the water. Each category has a range of 0–25, far too wide to be of any real use.

A cheap but effective solution—if the appraisal is a paper-based system, simply draw a line under the four boxes and make that a 1 to 100 scale and get the managers to simply indicate on the line the appropriate score. From Chapter 2 you will recall we are collecting productivity information from three prime sources:

- Competency
- Performance
- Reliability

Each of these scores will appear for each individual so that we can do predictions, by individual, by department or for the organization.

Software to use

The internationally accepted software is to use a Monte Carlo simulator. This makes the whole job quick and easy. Various packages exist, all of which do the same job, but they vary in price from $100 to $5,000 plus.

1. Example 1

   When doing predictive calculations it is important to remember that the information must add value to the organization and have with it a recommendation or advice.

   In this example we are looking at an organization that employs 13,000 people. We are specifically interested in the competency levels.

   The data used has come from performance appraisal scores and has been stored in an Excel spreadsheet by departments. We know from the presets shown in Chapter 4 that the required average is 75 percent. In this example the data had been reported, but it was buried in a mass of other statistics every year, but nothing had been done about it.

   Once you can see the prediction, you can recognize the problem. The competency level is nowhere near the required 70 percent. Further examination of other related data showed there were less investment in training during this period and an increase in the accident rate within the company, and that turnover had also steadily increased.

Year	Competency (organizational) as a percentage
1995	70
1996	65
1997	68
1998	60
1999	64
2000	71
2001	72
2002	61
2003	64
2004	68
2005	61
2006	69
2007	67
2008	69
2009	67
2010	62
2011	67
2012	67

Recommendation, if the 70 percent is still to be the company average competency level then an increase in the level of competency-based training is needed, the cost of which would be justified by a lower turnover rate of 3 percent and reduced accident rate.

2. Example Sysco

Sysco, like many other companies in the world, was looking to improve efficiency. They undertook a study to determine what impact the cost of turnover was having on their business. At the time of the survey and projection their turnover rate was about average, but increasing, particularly in their lorry delivery area. The extract below is from an interview with Ken Carring; once he had identified the problem and then taken action, the benefits speak for themselves.

Ken Carring, Senior Vice President and Chief Administrative Officer:

"75% of SYSCO's costs are people related expenses and for us what that means is about three billion dollars of expenses and so when we can move retention of our marketing associates, of which we have about ten thousand marketing associates, if we can move that retention rate from 70% to 80%, for us, that means approximately, with ten thousand marketing associates, that's approximately $50 thousand per marketing associate, turns out to be over $70 million of savings per year.

Since 1998 we've moved our marketing associate retention from 70% to 82%. Our delivery associates, which are a very critical success to SYSCO because they know the customers, they're the ones that the customers rely on getting their groceries to them on time and in the condition that they expected and in order to get them on time you need to have the same person going to the same customer on a regular basis.

For us, we were able to move our delivery associates from about 65% retention rate to 85% and we've costed out the training and hiring loss for delivery associates to be about $35 thousand, so again, almost another $50 million in savings when we made that kind of contribution, which for SYSCO investors that's about every 5 million, is a penny per share, so there's 10 cents right there."

3. Example BMW 2016

   We did some work with BMW. They did a number of projections relating to the age of its workforce. It showed that it had an ageing workforce (unusual for the automotive industry). Productivity increases were planned and the challenge was how to make an ageing workforce more productive.

   Rather than think of removing or replacing its ageing workforce BMW asked a simple but very effective question to its older workers

   What do you need to help you work better?

   What happened?

   • The decision was made to help the older people to work better by changing their working environment.
   • How much did this cost?
     ○ Wooden flooring   Euro 5,000.00
     ○ Barbershop-type chairs   Euro 1,000.00
     ○ Orthopedic footwear   Euro 2,000.00
     ○ Angled monitors with large print   Euro No cost
     ○ Magnifying lenses   Euro 1,000.00

○ Adjustable work tables	No cost
○ Large handled gripping tools	No cost—How?
○ Stackable transport containers	No cost
○ Manual hoisting cranes	Euro 1,000.00
○ Management time to run project	Euro 10,000.00
Total cost plus salary	Euro 50,000

The result

In the area where this was done productivity went up by 7 percent and sickness dropped to below the factory average.

Clearly not all of the benefits could be attributed to workforce planning, but in all three examples it shows the power of predictive techniques.

6.7   Predictive Forecasting for Growth

One of the traditional formulas still used by workforce planners for predictive forecasting does not work in practice. The half life cycle formula has been replaced by predictive software and a better understanding of key indicators. It's important for all predictive forecasting to understand how the business works and what the link is between work done and support needed. These ratios must be worked out in a sound and methodical way, as the data becomes the foundation for accurate forecasting.

A) First establish the right size of the organization using **FORMULA 9**. You might not use this information straightaway, you do need to factor it in for long-term forecasting.

B) Next establish key workload figures. This does apply not only to the private sector, but to any organization. First find out what the key production people produce each day. A good example of this is in the case study Lane Engineering. Here we have established that production workers produce 17 units per person per day and packing works each pack 25.5 units per person each day.

C) Once workloads have been established it very straightforward to calculate how many support staff are needed to make the organization work effectively.

Now that you have the information it's very straightforward to be able to do a predictive chart that will show how many people are needed to support any future growth plans. The added value is that you will be able to get the gearing ratios spot on.

N.B. With expansion and contraction you have to factor in the three types of employees—this factor must also be used when forecasting from predictable wastage.

You need to know what category of employee is leaving or is being replaced. For example, if (based on the 2010 survey) you had 10 poor performers leaving—it is likely that their work could be done by just three average performers—it is vital that you know the percentages of poor performers, average performers, and high performers when doing any of the expansion or contraction calculations. This must be worked out for your own organization so that all your workforce forecasting can be accurate.

In the past many forecasting mistakes have been made based on the assumption that employees all work the hours they are paid for—this is simply not true and we need to take a very pragmatic view on this.

The survey which was completed late in 2014/2015 showed that

Poor performers worked for 5 hours a week and accounted for 17 percent of the workforce.

Average performers worked for 22 hours a week and accounted for 61 percent of the workforce.

High performers worked for 32 hours a week and accounted for 22 percent of the workforce.

The survey was carried out in the Middle East, specifically large companies—110 in total—and focused on real work hours.

If you think these figures are unbelievable, in 2017, both the Saudi newspaper and the *Times* reported on a story that most people employed in the Public sector worked less than 60 minutes a day.

6.8   Predictive Forecasting for Contraction

The biggest fault I have seen in contraction circumstances—particularly in the world financial crisis—is the delay and reluctance to take action. This has been the downfall of many large and successful organizations.

We witnessed Kodak, a world brand name, file for bankruptcy protection and Nokia stock referred to as "junk status" in the financial press.

It has also been apparent that the old style manpower planning departments seem to have been caught on their backfoot focusing on the wrong or inappropriate data.

Actions that need to be taken are very similar for growth with the exception of the positioning of formula 9. Formula 9 is the trigger and the absolute minimum number to work with. From experience, most organizations we have worked with have reduced by 20 percent without an undue strain on the organization.

Using Richards Engineering as an example it's very obvious that a massive saving in staff numbers lies not with the workers but in the areas of management and auxiliary support. As with growth it's easy to sort out the right numbers for any reduction in production brought about by declining market demand.

6.9 Formulas and Unit Costs (The 10 Key Formula)

Dr. Tony Miller's formulas for organisational efficiency – 2017/18

Days Worked—Prime Working Days Formula 10 PWD

In nearly all Partnership Planning work sooner or later you will need this calculation. How many days do people actually work in your organization, normal reply 365, but it's not true, so how many days does your human resource work? The calculation will vary from company to company; an acknowledged average is 226 days a year. When you use the formula you will need to adjust the figures for an exact fit for your company.

Days in the year 365 − (Holidays 25 + Public Holidays 10 + Weekends 104) = 226 PWD

Formula 10

The figure of 226 becomes the amount of days for productivity calculations, business expansion, or contraction calculations and the basis of calculating the employee standard unit cost (ESUC).

What Is the ESUC for Days Actually Worked?—Formula 5

The ESUC is the basis of all calculations for efficiency, production, costs and efficiency savings. This is one very emotive figure, once you understand how it's calculated then run it past the finance Director to get the figure approved—remember this is a rough unit cost, it's an average—not an exact figure. It's good enough for us to do a range of calculations and predictions.

A worked example of formula 5:

This is a company that employs 3,000 people with a total salary bill that includes salaries, overtime, car allowance, housing allowance, and ALL allowances including medical and any tax contributions. In this example, it amounts to £125,280,000.00. You will see on the calculation that the total salary costs are multiplied by 2. Two is our real expenses we can attribute to every employee training, electricity, facilities, IT, floor space, company vehicles, etc.

If you have lots of spare time, you can work this out by looking at the annual accounts (private sector only) but for simplicity we use 2 as the factor. There are a few companies where the factor would be higher such a Google, Apple, Facebook, etc.

Remember you are not the company mathematics department—you just need working standard figures.

We then divide the top line total by the number of employees which gives us X.

ESUC. To find the Unit cost for any employee per day

Part 1

Total salary + associated costs £125,280,000.00 × 2= £83,520 X

No. of employees 3,000

X is then divided by 226 (PWD) to give you the ESUC per day, which is the true cost of each employee in the organization.

$$\frac{X£83,520}{226} = \text{ESUC } £369$$

divide by 8 (depending on country) to get hour rate £46.

Understanding these two formulas 5 and 12 enables you to take a hard look at what people do in the time they are actually available for work.

I have experienced little comment on calculating the PWD, but the ESUC always seems very controversial, often the comment from CFOs is that it not the way we do it—my reply is always the same to this statement—"well please show me the formula you use" —of course there is none.

How Much Does Appraisal Cost—Formula 6

Performance appraisal is one of the most costly, time–intensive, and disliked process inflicted by HR. Ask HR how much their process costs—don't hold your breath while waiting for the reply. The fact is that properly run performance appraisal is essential particularly for workforce planners. It gives us two of our three critical pieces of management information—competency scores and performance scores. So like it or hate it—we need it.

Cost of a performance appraisal for a normal (not 360) appraisal

TH × TE × ESUC = annual cost of yearly appraisal

where TH is the total hours spent including all processing time

TE is the total number of employees

ESUC is the unit cost per hour of each employee.

So let's examine the cost of appraisal for a company employing 5,000 people with an average employee unit cost of £46 per hour.

For each appraisal

Appraiser's time preparing 0.5 hours × £46	£23.00
Appraisee's time preparing 0.5 hours × £46	£23.00
Appraisal time for appraiser 1 × £46	£46.00
Appraisal time appraisee 1 × £46	£46.00
After the appraisal—completing documentation appraise 0.5 hours × £46	£23.00
After the appraisal—talking and reflecting appraise 0.5 hours × £46	£23.00
HR processing time for each appraisal 0.5 hours × £46	£23.00
Subtotal	£207.00
3,000 employees × £207	£621,000.00

In addition it would be fair to add the cost of misdirected training identified from appraisal. This could be as high as 70 percent of the training budget—the cost of which would need to be added to the calculation.

In our example we have a cost to the business of £621,000.00—to get just a simple return on investment we need to get each year £621,000.00 of measurable bottom line benefits. Can your appraisal system deliver this type of performance?

If you go beyond return on investment to seek added value then it would be reasonable to expect to see a 20 percent added value each year. In other words each year the system is in place, we should expect to see minimum measurable benefits of £745,200.00. Can your system deliver this type of business performance?

HR and Training ROI Formula 8

AV (actual business value created in one year) − total cost of activity = added value (or loss)

This is a very simple formula used to measure added value. It's particularly relevant to Workforce planners in the New Workforce planning arena as the value created is so high it would be the basis of making the department a profit center in its own right.

A recent example of creating added value is the BMW case study shown in this book.

Value created 7 percent improvement in productivity + reduction in sickness – the process costs

50,000 Euro = ROI added value

Due to confidentiality restrictions regretfully I can't reveal to you the value of the two benefits in BMW but as an example these figures are very substantial and very significant.

How Many People Do You Need to Run the Organization? Formula 10

During the present world difficulties, the question most often asked by CEOs and CFOs is how many people do we really need to run the organization?

The question then that needs to be asked is "Is all of the planned work being completed?" The answer most of the time is a rather reluctant one—but it's yes in most cases. If that is so then certain assumptions can be made and following formula can be deployed to get a gauge for the right size needed for the organization.

Total staff employed × PWD – (training days and Reliability total days) = Man days needed to run the organization

The result is one of fact—that's how many man-days were needed. There is no suggestion that people can't be off sick or that the training should stop, but the figure gives you a base line to work from.

In the Western world during 2011 and 2012, in many organizations rightsized reductions of 20 percent have been common with little if any detrimental effect to the function of the organization.

You can further refine the figures by looking at the percentage in the organization of poor and average performers. These examples are in Chapter 4 in the section on Performance.

A full step-by-step example of how to do this is in Chapter 4.

Calculating Average Competency Levels

This is not really a significant formula, rather a straightforward mathematical calculation. It's in this section as it's the one calculation where most mistakes are made. The example just shows the mathematical process.

This calculation would be used for the three prime Productivity indicators: Competency, Performance, and Reliability.

Example

2,000 staff at 55% competence	= 110,000
1,000 × 70% competence	= 70,000
total	180,000

Divide the 180,000 by 3,000 (no of staff) = 60 Company average competency this year 60%

Missing Formulas

Lots—most don't work, many others have just been replaced with appropriate software packages. One of my favorite tools as a consultant is one devised by the late Dr. Michael Hammer: F.A.C.E.

It is Fast, it is Accurate, it is Cheap to use, and it is Easy to use. This is a very useful concept to keep in your mind when being a Business Partner. Focus on matters that will make a difference to organizational efficiency—get the big picture—keep focus at strategic level—that's where the big gains are made.

CHAPTER 7

The HR Business Partner in Action Case Study

7.1   A Quick Recap

So far in the book we have looked at:

- The design of HR to be effective beyond 2017
- How the HR strategic model works
- The specific skills needed to be an HR Business Partner
- Some of the processes that you need to master
- The importance of showing results in monetary terms
- Throughout the book we have stressed the need for creativity and innovation

What exactly does the HR business partner do on a regular basis and how does the job work in practice?

7.2   Putting HR the Business Partner into Practice

Based on a 2017 oil industry example, company size + 20,000 employees.

Background

The company is a large employer employing over 20,000 staff. The HR function is centralized but has HR personnel based at each of the five main site offices. The role of the site-based staff is to provide day-to-day HR support, although this is more like routine clerical HR assistance to the site managers. The company embraced the concept of HR as a business partner but struggled to implement it in the company due to the misunderstanding of what the role involved.

Getting Started

The first hurdle to overcome is how many HR business partners do you need? With five big site offices and a very large central function, how many people will be needed?

In reality its quite small: five people were all that was needed. Most of the existing HR employees wanted to do this job, unaware of the specialist skills that would be needed.

Where Would the Business Partner Staff Be Based?

It's a central function. If you look at the time split, with 20 percent of the time with the allocated area and the remaining 80 percent in central HR, it means pooling and drawing together resources to provide innovative solutions to organizational issues.

7.3   The Skillset Needed

We have already discussed (Section 1.5) the skill set needed to work as a matrix consultant. In addition, there are some key competencies that are essential if the person is going to be a successful business partner.

Innovation and creativity
Calculating and producing financial benefit presentations
Mastery of key management processes
Understanding and being able to use Business Process Re-engineering
   tools
Workforce Planning

These are critical competencies in addition to being a competent HR professional. When interviewing for this position, the Company ran an assessment center to test all of the above.

7.4   Some Examples of the Successful Work of a HR Business Partner

Downsizing and Rightsizing

Rightsizing is a very useful way to help the management rescope on how many people are needed—coupled with this would be re-engineering the organizational design. This can be done department by department, which makes the possibility of getting this done and achieving success much better. In a recent rightsizing exercise company staff costs were reduced by 20 percent.

Business Process Re-engineering

The HR Business partner will need to understand and be able to do business process re-engineering and to be able to work out the cost benefit. We do a one-day program that gives this transfer of skills.

Some basic facts—processes deteriorate over time and sometimes the reason for the process becomes lost with time. IT innovations always impact on processes but often we see the IT innovation with little if any change to the process, missing a great opportunity. This is explained in my 2017 book "HR Analytics and Innovations in Workforce Planning."

With any process then being examined you should constantly question if the process adds value, whether or not it is relevant, or can it be scrapped altogether. Such an HR process to look at is Performance appraisal—in its present form, does it add measurable value?

Richard Branson of the Virgin group recently scrapped keeping holiday records, and the entire holiday system process. He had worked out that the cost of maintaining such a system had no significant financial benefit.

BPR provides a massive return on investment and it's very straightforward measuring the financial benefits to the business. The HR business partner is in exactly the right space to be able to spot what's needed.

Watching

You can learn a lot from watching what's going on. A company in the Middle East had a request for 15 additional staff in their Operations functions. The HR Business partner had observed a number of factors that were affecting productivity. In discussion with the manager various alterations were made, resulting in only 1 extra employee being needed.

Critical Thinking

A large manufacturing company in Germany had received an order that would mean production had to move from 10,000 units a day to 15,000 units. The HR partner working with the production manager and packaging manager redesigned the workflow and by relocating employees between departments was able to provide the right staff in the right place at the right time to successfully meet the production needs.

Bibliography

Advances in Strategy – Harvard Business Review on Advances in Strategy Review (2002).

Auer Antoncic, J., & Antoncic, B. (2011). Employee satisfaction, intrapreneurship and firm growth: A model. Industrial Management & Data Systems, 111(4), 589–607.

Bloom, N., & Van Reenen, J. (2011). Human resource management and productivity. Handbook of Labor Economics, 4, 1697–1767.

Böckerman, P., & Ilmakunnas, P. (2012). The job satisfaction-productivity nexus: A study using matched survey and register data. Industrial & Labor Relations Review, 65(2), 244–262.

Boehm, J. K., & Lyubomirsky, S. (2008). Does happiness promote career success? Journal of Career Assessment, 16(1), 101–116.

Bozionelos, N. (2005). When the inferior candidate is offered the job: The selection interview as a political and power game. Human Relations, 58(12), 1605–1631.

Brtek, M. D., & Motowildo, S. J. (2002). Effects of procedure and outcome accountability on interview validity. Journal of Applied Psychology, 87, 185–191.

Burney, L. L., Henle, C. A., & Widener, S. K. (2009). A path model examining the relations among strategic performance measurement system characteristics, organizational justice, and extra-and in-role performance. Accounting, Organizations and Society, 34(3), 305–321.

Charan R. – Know How

CIPD People Management Magazine UK T. Swart (7 2014) – Article The Neuroscience of Bias

Collins J. (2001). Good to Great. New York: Harper Business.

Creasy, T., & Anantatmula, V. S. (2013). From every direction – How personality traits and dimensions of project managers can conceptually affect project success. Project Management Journal, 44(6), 36–51.

Fisher, C. D. (2010). Happiness at work. International journal of management reviews, 12(4), 384-412. Hosie, P., Willemyns, M., & Sevastos, P. (2012). The impact of happiness on managers' contextual and task performance. Asia Pacific Journal of Human Resources, 50(3), 268–287.

Franco-Santos, M., Lucianetti, L., & Bourne, M. (2012). Contemporary performance measurement systems: A review of their consequences and a framework for research. Management Accounting Research, 23(2), 79–119.

Furnham, A., Miller, T, Batey, M., & Johnson S. (2012). Demographic and individual correlates of self-rated competency. Unknown Journal, 31(3), 247–265.

Grafton, J., Lillis, A. M., & Widener, S. K. (2010). The role of performance measurement and evaluation in building organizational capabilities and performance. Accounting, Organizations and Society, 35(7), 689–706.

Hall, M. (2008). The effect of comprehensive performance measurement systems on role clarity, psychological empowerment and managerial performance. Accounting, Organizations and Society, 33(2), 141–163.

Hamilton, R. T. (2011). How firms grow and the influence of size and age. International Small Business Journal, 29(3), 278–294.

Hansen, B., & Hamilton, R. T. (2011). Factors distinguishing small firm growers and non-growers. International Small Business Journal, 29(3), 278–294.

Hiam A. – The Vest Pocket CEO – Decision Making Tools for Executives

Kim Chan W. & Mauborgne R – Blue OceanStrategy (2015) Harvard Business School

Hesselbein F. & Johnston R. – On High Performance Organizations (2002) The Drucker Foundation

McLean, R. D., & Zhao, M. (2014). The business cycle, investor sentiment, and costly external finance. The Journal of Finance, 69(3), 1377–1409.

Miller T. Dr (2017). HR Analytics and Innovations in workforce planning. BEP

Miller T. Dr (2017). Successful Interviewing -a talent -focused approach to successful recruitment and selection BEP

Miller, T (2015). Latest Techniques in Workforce Planning

Miller, T. (2012). NEW HR

Miller, T. (2011). The HR Dashboard, Wolters Kluwer International Publication

Miller, T. (2014). Added value HR Croners Publications

Miller, T. (2014). Downsizing and Right sizing – Croners Publications

Miller, T. (2015) Successful Interviewing

Miller, T. (2015). Differentiation for Talent Management (in Russian) – BizEducation

Miller, T. (2015). How to Rightsize (Russian) BizEducate

Miller, T. (2015). HR Process Re-Engineering – Wolters Kluwer International Publication

Miller, T. (2015). New Techniques in Workforce Planning

Miller, T. (2015). Successful Interviewing – A Process Approach

Miller, T. (2015). The New HR strategic Map – Croners Publications

Oswald, A. J., Proto, E., & Sgroi, D. (2009). Happiness and productivity. IZA Discussion Paper No. 4645. Bonn: Institute for the study of Labor.

Van Reenen, J. (2011). Does competition raise productivity through improving management quality? International Journal of Industrial Organization, 29(3), 306–316.

Winning, Welch J and Welch S (2005) HarperT orch Zelenski, J. M., Murphy, S. A., & Jenkins, D. A. (2008). The happy-productive worker thesis revisited. Journal of Happiness Studies, 9(4), 521–537.

HR Department Maturity Questionnaire

This questionnaire is designed to establish the maturity of your HR Department. The maturity of a department is not determined by the maturity of the individuals within it, but reflects the focus of the department and the type of work in which it is engaged.

The factors considered in this instrument for rating the maturity of your department are: RECRUITMENT; APPRAISAL; PAY, TERMS, AND CONDITIONS; INFORMATION MANAGEMENT; ORGANIZATIONAL CHANGE; TRAINING & DEVELOPMENT

You are asked to consider the individual behavioral indicators and descriptors within each column and decide which COLUMN of descriptors is most characteristic of your department. You are likely to find that some descriptors from different columns apply to your department but are asked to select the column that is most characteristic. You should rate this honestly and not respond with how you would like it to be, or how you think your organization should be.

Example

Organizational Change

The focus of our department with regard to Organizational Change can typically be characterized as:

Respond to calls for organizational change from the line—inform on implications such as headcount and impact on staffing budget	Advise managers on best way to implement changes to roles, working practices, and terms and conditions	Work on HR impact of business process re-engineering and the need to develop key staff to cope	Suggest restructuring and radical organizational change as part of developing business strategy
Ensure legal responsibilities are not compromised	Work with line managers to ensure any changes to current practice are implemented within the law while minimizing cost to the business	Highlight the need for change in competencies and approach and work with line managers to embed these	Act as "corporate conscience" on defining and living the values—feedback to all those not acting in keeping with these
Handle questions from individuals with regard to the likely impact of change on their personal circumstances	Work with managers to overcome concerns about implementing change in their areas	Deal with conflict between managers over the implementation of change and potentially negative impact of one area on another	Drive change that impacts directly on the business outside of HR specific concerns
☐	☑	☐	☐

Recruitment

The focus of our Department with regard to Recruiting can typically be characterized as:

Plan recruitment once notified by the business that there is a need to recruit	Invited by the business to advise them how to approach a recruitment need	Liaise with the business to anticipate their need to recruit	Determine recruitment plans as part of the strategic business planning process	☐
Target recruitment on the basis of a job title and a salary range	Work with the business to define a Job Specification to guide recruitment	Work with the business to define a Job and Person Specification to guide recruitment	Supplement the Job and Person Specification with an exploration of future demands and business direction to guide recruitment	
Draft advertisements to attract candidates	Employ agencies to draft advertisements and/or find potential candidates	Employ search firms to find prospective candidates and advertise internally	Apply a range of methods for locating potential candidates, e.g., subsidiaries, secondments, internet	☐
Interview candidates	Interview and use psychometric tests in some instances	Train or coach line managers on interviewing skills and use assessment centers for managerial posts	Utilize customized state-of-the-art assessment procedures at all levels	
Take responsibility for organization of interviews and the drafting of offer letters	Take responsibility for information provided for hiring managers in addition to organization of the process	Take responsibility for quality of the assessment process and its organization	Take responsibility for the overall effectiveness of recruitment and assessment decisions	☐
Ensure new starters are registered on all HR systems	Encourage the business to provide a structured induction for new starters	Organize the induction for new starters	Organize and monitor the effectiveness of induction for new starters and intervene to resolve issues or make improvements	☐

Appraisal

The focus of our department with regard to Appraisal can typically be characterized as:

Encourage appraisal of performance to underpin recommendations on remuneration	Manage a formal annual appraisal process based on performance against objectives	Manage a formal annual appraisal process based on performance against objectives and some behavioral criteria. Provide briefing for managers	Manage a formal annual appraisal process based on performance against objectives, behavioral competencies, and corporate values. Both brief and train managers extensively on process
Log recommendations for pay awards from line managers	Record the levels of performance against objectives achieved within the business in the form of appraisal ratings	Record the levels of performance against objectives and behavioral criteria achieved within the business and document individual development needs	Record the levels of achievement attained against objectives, competencies, and behavior and evaluations of future potential. Collate this information to gauge and publicize corporate capability
Issue timely reminders that pay reviews need to be conducted	Monitor the level of appraisal returns from within the business	Monitor the distribution of appraisal ratings across the business	Identify and act upon weak spots in managerial appraisal providing feedback and assistance to improve
Action recommendations on pay awards	Advise on development options available to managers looking to develop key staff	Follow up on priority development needs emerging from appraisals	Formulate individual and corporate development plans as part of succession planning, highlighting vulnerabilities
☐	☐	☐	☐

Pay, Terms, and Conditions

The focus of our department with regard to Pay, Terms, and Conditions can typically be characterized as:

Administer an off-the-shelf or part manual payroll system	Administer a part-customized payroll system capable of modification by in-house remuneration experts	Oversee purpose-built, fully customizable payroll system	Largely outsourced payroll system flexibly modified on request
Remuneration is predominantly salary based within the organization	Remuneration features some benefits and company bonus scheme	Remuneration includes multiple benefits and personal bonus based on company and individual performance	Reward schemes enhance typical remuneration strategies offering flexible packages tied in to business, team, and individual performance
Use historical data to set levels of remuneration and adapt these according to market conditions	Research pay surveys to ensure remuneration is in line with the market and demands of specialists	Link pay to performance wherever possible maximizing elements such as bonuses and profit-related pay	Link pay and reward directly to value add to the business
Pay increases determined by reference to inflation and typically "flat rate"	Pay increases and bonus determined by company performance	Pay increases determined by personal and company performance	Rewards fully flexible to accommodate exceptional input and acknowledge contribution to team and to the wider organization
☐	☐	☐	☐

Information Management

The focus of our department with regard to Information Management can typically be characterized as:

Repository for basic biographic detail about staff	Maintain records on staff work history and experience	Retain and update records on individual work performance and history	Manage a system that captures detailed information about individual performance, aspirations, and competence	☐
IT Development targets storage capacity and speed of processing	IT Development targets extending the range of data held and its accessibility	IT Development targets functionality and reporting capability	IT Development targets creation of expert system and predictive/modeling capability	☐
Information accessed for routine purposes or in response to specific requests from senior managers	Information accessed for standard reports, e.g., headcount, etc., and in response to managerial requests	Information produced to supplement business reports and to support decision making; intranet provides contact details and HR news	Information synthesized to create succession plans and model what–if scenarios; controlled open access to data via intranet available and this developed to answer frequently asked questions and advice	☐
Separate systems maintained for different aspects of HR work	Periodic updates of information and database cleaning planned to minimize discrepancies in information held	Systems updated regularly and data managed actively	Fully integrated systems allowing rapid updates and communication between databases	☐

Organizational Change

The focus of our department with regard to Organizational Change can typically be characterized as:

Respond to calls for organizational change from the line – inform on implications such as headcount and impact on staffing budget Ensure legal responsibilities are not compromised Handle questions from individuals with regard to the likely impact of change on their personal circumstances	Advise on best way to implement changes to roles, working practices, and terms and conditions Work with line managers to ensure any changes to current practice are implemented within the law while minimizing cost to the business Work with managers to overcome concerns about implementing change in their areas	Work on HR impact of business process re-engineering and the need to develop key staff to cope Highlight the need for change in competencies and approach and work with line managers to embed these Deal with conflict between managers over the implementation of change and potentially negative impact of one area on another	Suggest restructuring and radical organizational change as part of developing business strategy Act as "corporate conscience" on defining and living the values—feedback to all those not acting in keeping with these Drive change that impacts directly on the business outside of HR-specific concerns
☐	☐	☐	☐

Training and Development

The focus of our department with regard to Training & Development can typically be characterized as:

Administer training budget and assist managers in finding course to meet specific training needs Fund training in response to specific requests from line managers Use external training professionals or in-house experts to teach staff Take note of dissatisfaction or criticism of training providers to update and amend list	Agree training budgets as part of review of training needs with departments Publish a prospectus of courses available from which managers may select Deliver the bulk of training through in-house trainers using externals for specialist courses Canvass delegate opinion to monitor satisfaction with training provided	Advise managers on options available to meet training needs identified through appraisal Obtain business case from managers in support of requests for training Utilize external trainers to supplement own resource or deliver on high-profile programs Conduct trials and observe courses directly to evaluate their effectiveness	Determine training and development priorities based on appraisal information in the context of business strategy Training and development strategy determined for the business as integral part of strategic business planning Maintain a preferred supplier resource pool and partner with them to design and deliver training and development programs Measure directly the impact of training and development on performance to evaluate and improve course content and delivery
☐	☐	☐	☐

HR Department Maturity Questionnaire Scoring Guide

Transcribe your scores for each section into the corresponding boxes below and add up the number of ticks in each column

RECRUITMENT

☐ ☐ ☐ ☐

APPRAISAL

☐ ☐ ☐ ☐

PAY, TERMS, AND

☐ ☐ ☐ ☐

CONDITIONS

☐ ☐ ☐ ☐

INFORMATION MANAGEMENT

☐ ☐ ☐ ☐

ORGANIZATIONAL CHANGE

☐ ☐ ☐ ☐

TRAINING & DEVELOPMENT

☐ ☐ ☐ ☐

TOTAL

The largest total indicates the most characteristic column for your department

To plot your position calculate the following:

TOTAL

$$\boxed{} \times 1 \quad + \quad \boxed{} \times 2 \quad + \quad \boxed{} \times 3 \quad + \quad \boxed{} \times 4$$

TOTAL =_____

'80's HR	'90's HR	'2000' HR	'Business Partner' HR
6 | 7 | 8 | 9	10 | 11 | 12 | 13 | 14 | 15	16 | 17 | 18 | 19 | 20	21 | 22 | 23 | 24

This is a great tool for finding out where you are now and can be used to brief others in the training function about the need to change/improve. It's particularly interesting to compare how your customers (managers and directors) see you compared to how you see your own department.

APPENDIX 1

Here we are looking to see what the relationship is between students who do well at maths and science—is there any relationship? Let's find out.

Example 1: Data

Student:	Maths (X):	Science (Y):	X^2	Y^2	X*Y
A	11	11	$11^2 -$	$11^2 -$	–
B	13	10	$13^2 -$	$10^2 -$	–
C	18	17	$18^2 -$	$17^2 -$	–
D	12	13	$12^2 -$	$13^2 -$	–
E	16	14	$16^2 -$	$14^2 -$	–
N=	Ilx=	I'y =	$IIX^2 =$	$I' Y^2=$	IIXY=

Have a go and see if you can do it!

Example 1: Complete Data Table

Student:	Maths (X):	Science (Y):	X^2	Y^2	X*Y
A	11	11	$11^2 = 121$	$11^2 = 121$	11*11 = 121
B	13	10	$13^2 = 169$	$10^2 = 100$	13*10 = 130
C	18	17	$18^2 = 324$	$17^2 = 289$	18*17 = 306
D	12	13	$12^2 = 144$	$13^2 = 169$	12*13 = 156
E	16	14	$16^2 = 256$	$14^2 = 196$	16*14 = 224
N = 5	Dx = 70	I\r = 65	Ilxz =1014	$IJY^2 =875$	IIXY = 937

Hope you got it right!

Example 1: Equation

$$r = \frac{IXY - \frac{(IX) * (IY)}{N}}{\sqrt{\left[\Sigma X^2 - \frac{(\Sigma X)^2}{N}\right] * \left[\Sigma Y^2 - \frac{(\Sigma Y)^2}{N}\right]}}$$

Put in the numbers.

Example 1: Step One—Put In The Numbers

$$r = \frac{937 - \frac{(70) * (65)}{5}}{\left[1014 - \frac{(70)^2}{5}\right] * \left[875 - \frac{(65)^2}{5}\right]}$$

Do the math!

Example 1: Step Two—Do The Maths

$$r = \frac{937 - 910}{\sqrt{(1014 - 980) * (875 - 845)}}$$

Example 1: Step Three—Finish The Calculation

$$r = \frac{27}{\sqrt{34 * 30}} \qquad r = \frac{27}{31.937438}$$

ANSWER: r = .8454028
r = 0.845

In this word, there is a strong positive correlation between student's marks in math and science. So what's the added value comment?

All that's needed is just one test–for the company concerned it was a massive financial saving.

This practical book is yet another in the series of transitioning HR functions into the mainline business.

Written by the well-established international author Dr Tony Miller.

Index

OTHER TITLES IN THE HUMAN RESOURCE MANAGEMENT AND ORGANIZATIONAL BEHAVIOR COLLECTION

- *The Illusion of Inclusion: Global Inclusion, Unconscious Bias, and the Bottom Line* by Helen Turnbull
- *On All Cylinders: The Entrepreneur's Handbook* by Ron Robinson
- *Employee LEAPS: Leveraging Engagement by Applying Positive Strategies* by Kevin E. Phillips
- *Making Human Resource Technology Decisions: A Strategic Perspective* by Janet H. Marler and Sandra L. Fisher
- *Feet to the Fire: How to Exemplify And Create The Accountability That CreatesGreat Companies* by Lorraine A. Moore
- *HR Analytics and Innovations in Workforce Planning* by Tony Miller
- *Deconstructing Management Maxims, Volume I: A Critical Examination of Conventional Business Wisdom* by Kevin Wayne
- *Deconstructing Management Maxims, Volume II: A Critical Examination of Conventional Business Wisdom* by Kevin Wayne
- *The Real Me: Find and Express Your Authentic Self* by Mark Eyre
- *Across the Spectrum: What Color Are You?* by Stephen Elkins-Jarrett
- *Life of a Lifetime: Inspiration for Creating Your Extraordinary Life* by Christoph Spiessens
- *The Facilitative Leader: Managing Performance Without Controlling People* by Steve Reilly
- *The Human Resource Professional's Guide to Change Management: Practical Tools and Techniques to Enact Meaningful and Lasting Organizational Change* by Melanie J. Peacock
- *Tough Calls: How to Move Beyond Indecision and Good Intentions* by Linda D. Henman

Announcing the Business Expert Press Digital Library

Concise e-books business students need for classroom and research

This book can also be purchased in an e-book collection by your library as

- *a one-time purchase,*
- *that is owned forever,*
- *allows for simultaneous readers,*
- *has no restrictions on printing, and*
- *can be downloaded as PDFs from within the library community.*

Our digital library collections are a great solution to beat the rising cost of textbooks. E-books can be loaded into their course management systems or onto students' e-book readers. The **Business Expert Press** digital libraries are very affordable, with no obligation to buy in future years. For more information, please visit **www.businessexpertpress.com/librarians**. To set up a trial in the United States, please email **sales@businessexpertpress.com**.

www.ingramcontent.com/pod-product-compliance
Lightning Source LLC
Chambersburg PA
CBHW071844200326
41519CB00016B/4233